Victory Beyond the Scoreboard

Building Winners in Life
Through Youth Sports

John Devine and Cliff Gillies

BookPartners, Inc.
Wilsonville, Oregon

BookPartners, Inc.
P.O. Box 922
Wilsonville, Oregon 97070

Dedication

To Brian, Connor, Jamie, Kelsey, Lauren, MacKenzie, Nathan, Phillip and Robert, and all the players, parents, and coaches who have inspired us to write a definitive book on the true value of participation.

Acknowledgments

To our wives, Sally and Dianne, the co-leaders of all our aspirations.

To our children, Ann, Catherine, Don, Erin, Maureen, Pat, Scott and Susan, and their spouses whose victories in life are all we ever wanted. We thank you for your support while we attended to the matters of the community's youth.

We gratefully acknowledge all conscientious coaches, activity directors, and officials who realize that it is through our combined efforts that we are able to do the greatest amount of good for the largest number of tomorrow's leaders.

We congratulate everyone who has competed with honor to win beyond the scoreboard, for it was you who patiently and effectively resolved issues and injustices for the betterment of future participants.

We are grateful for the opportunity to know the young people who played on our teams and their parents. Your enthusiasm injected an exuberance for life. You taught us lessons about acceptance, respect, perseverance, and pure joy which far exceeded those you took from us.

A special thanks to four-time Olympian and our editor, Lyle Nelson; and his co-captains, Thorn and Ursula Bacon.

We acknowledge the unseen hand of our personal Coach, who has given us the opportunity to work with and for young people.

Table of Contents

Introduction

America needs a fresh look at sports. The Vince Lombardi approach, "Winning isn't everything — it's the only thing" does not have a place in youth sports. Only the top three percent of young athletes will become consistent winners and athletic stars. The "win-at-all-costs" philosophy neglects the other ninety-seven percent and, in fact, doesn't teach the right values to the winners either.

Learning lifelong values — values which are the behavioral foundation of honest workers, sensitive leaders, strong families, civic-minded neighbors, and capable parents — is the quintessential benefit of sports. Each contest, practice, meeting or moment of decision provides an opportunity for players to learn a skill, attitude or value that will reappear in their future. The success of any nation can be measured by the attitudes and behavior of its youth, not by their win-loss record. This book has been written to show parents how to build value into a sports program for their children, how to make informed choices from the menu of athletic activities, and how to select a program that is already value driven.

This book certainly is not meant to chastise coaches and programs. Most coaches are extremely devoted to serving youth and do a commendable job at great personal sacrifice and expense. Yet, the system can be and must be improved. An informed and active parent is the best insurance that emotional and physical abuse of youth, too often tolerated in the name of sport, can be eliminated.

The "stakeholders" in youth activities include coaches, players, parents, family members, relatives, teachers, league administrators, local boosters, business leaders, national sports organizations, local government and a seemingly endless list. All have vested interests and sometimes personal agendas for exerting influences on young athletes. The stakeholders, usually well-intended but frequently misinformed, on occasion impose expectations on youth that far exceed the intention of a learning experience. Should coaches who expect to win impose that same expectation upon eight-year-old players? Should a parent unconditionally relinquish a family member to a coach for five to twelve hours a week? What are the indicators that family values and parental control are becoming secondary rather than included? These questions, and many others, are answered in *Victory Beyond the Scoreboard.*

There is only one way to unite these diverse stakeholders and synchronize their contributions and expected payback (if any) from youth sports. The Partnership described in this book can vault youth sports into a new, truly supportive dimension.

It's difficult to escape noticing abhorrent examples of misconduct in sports. The media loves to spotlight outrageous behavior: the coach who assaults the umpire with a baseball bat makes the national news, but the majority of coaches who congratulate referees for calling a good game are seldom mentioned. Our craze over sports puts people in the spotlight, and serious infractions of rules catch a wide area of attention. Yet sports is still one of the safest and best personal growth activities for children, but parents must be vigilant for the infrequent abuses and they must know the right procedures for correcting them.

[Authors' Note: With respect and admiration, the authors throughout this book intend the term "parent" to include those adults who influence and are responsible for the social and educational well-being of young people.]

Assisting their children to make the right sports choices is an extremely important responsibility of parents. Coaches are second only to parents/guardians for influencing youths and invoking character attributes during the formative years. That is true whether the child participates in sports or not. Good coaches set high standards and expect everyone around them to live up to those standards. Just as you may spend considerable time evaluating a day-care facility for your child, it's important that you also evaluate who you are giving the responsibility to teach your child values on the playing field.

Showing parents how to make intelligent decisions while guiding their children through the youth sports maze is a central theme of this book. It will save parents time, money, and many moments of frustration. It will reduce the likelihood that their child will be a casualty of sports injustice.

One of the greatest benefits of youth sports is that it draws the family closer together. Any sports program that demands a greater allegiance to the team than to the family is ill-based. Vince Lombardi did get the order of important values in proper sequence when he said, "God, family and the Green Bay Packers." This book offers a well-tested model for using sports as the rallying activity that pulls families closer together.

This book represents the culmination of the authors' combined five decades of coaching and teaching kids, sports administration, and conducting workshops for coaches and parents. The overriding theme is to help young athletes grow into responsible and happy adults who have given of themselves and gained lifelong values in return. Knowing that you have chosen to be parents indicates that you share the same mission. We are confident that what you discover here will help you fulfill your obligations as a sports parent. Although imparting lifelong values and allowing kids to have fun through sports are stressed, they are not the only values; winning is not a four-letter word. If the right process is applied, and if the right values are followed, then winning becomes a by-product of doing the right things. This is the lesson that can be extracted from virtually all the great coaches in a variety of sports. Seldom do they emphasize the word "win," yet they consistently produce successful teams and individuals who win on and beyond the scoreboard.

Who will benefit from reading this book? Coaches will; they assist parents in determining their roles and responsibilities; all parents/guardians or extended family members with influence over young people in sports will benefit; as will professionals and volunteers who believe that sports is about more than being a winner on the scoreboard.

1

Sports: The Learning Field for Lifelong Values

If any proof were needed about the character-building aspects of sports, the story that follows by Luke Cyphers, reprinted with permission of *The Wall Street Journal,* is testimony to the values youngsters learn when they work together on a team. When it is led by a coach who understands the yearning of young people to be part of an exciting activity, the experience can make a lasting positive imprint on the lives of the players.

The Court of Angels

The Fort Washington armory is every bit as grim as you'd expect one of New York's largest and most dangerous homeless shelters to be. Hundreds of cots and dirty mattresses are shoved into the dingy corridors. Dead rats line the hall to the bathroom. Police are regular visitors.

But listen closely: One sound here doesn't belong. It's coming from behind the metal door of Room 23. It's the sound of squeaking sneakers.

Inside is another world — a brightly lit gym with a spit-shined hardwood floor. Sixteen seventh- and eighth-grade girls, none older than fourteen, are setting picks, running fast breaks and driving to the hoop as a muscular man with Groucho Marx eyebrows exhorts them to work still harder.

The Naturalness of Sport

All children are born with a natural affinity to play. As two-year-olds they completely exhaust parents as they crawl and jump into mischief. Energy is boundless. As soon as they become a little more surefooted, there are hills for them to run down, railroad tracks to walk on, playgrounds to explore and trees to climb. Given a physical challenge they attempt it, often without regard to peril. Children in this age group are determined little athletes: stubbing toes and bumping heads, and yet always bouncing back for more action.

This is the home court of the Incarnation School Angels, the Catholic Youth Organization girls' basketball champions of New York City. It is also the domain of the man with the eyebrows, Ted Staniecki, principal of the kindergarten-through-eighth-grade school, and the founder, driver, assistant coach, and all-around godfather of the team.

On the court, Sharon Paulino snares a missed shot away from Veronica Ayala as the two eighth-graders scrap for position under the basket.

"Veronica, get your butt down, your elbows out, and box her out of there," yells Mr. Staniecki. The girls scramble again, and this time Veronica forcefully backs Sharon away from the hoop. "That's it, Veronica," Mr. Staniecki calls. "Don't be afraid to be a little physical."

Perhaps the sharpest admonition you may have heard as a child was, "Would you just sit still, please?" In your heart, you knew that sitting still wasn't fun. Running, swinging, hanging or wrestling felt better. But you learned that if you wished to please your adult supervisors, you had better squelch your true desire for physical play until you had a chance to perform again!

Not just youth, but adults, too, have a natural affinity for physical play. As grueling as pioneer life was in the West a century ago, when time permitted, a group of wool-clad men and women in knee-high boots with makeshift equipment would, for reasons not entirely known even to themselves, set out to climb snowcapped mountains. In the established cities, inhabitants spent whole days waiting to get into games at the local park or schoolyard. Ancient Hawaiians surfed, Norwegians skied and Mongolians raced horses.

Over nearly two decades, the forty-one-year-old Mr. Staniecki has been helping children in the immigrant enclave of Washington Heights, giving them confidence, responsibility, and a will to win.

Few parents show up for Angels games: many are working, or simply can't afford trips across the city. The only parent who makes every game is the current head coach, George Lawrence, whose step-

daughter Niesha Butler is the Angels' star. Mr. Lawrence provides the strategy. Mr. Staniecki pushes the girls to dive for loose balls, pulls aside players who display a bad attitude, and generally holds things together.

Mr. Staniecki came late to basketball. The son of a Waldorf-Astoria Hotel doorman, he played football as a teenager in Queens, so when he started coaching basketball in 1975, it was literally by the book: "I'd go to the library to find books on rules, drills, everything."

Given idle time and good health, people worldwide will find outlets for physical play. In ancient Greece more than one hundred cities had recreational sports competitions. The most famous of these was held in Olympiad, and this tradition has been revived as the modern Olympic games.

But times change. In view of the findings in the Annual Report of the President's Council on Physical Fitness, you may doubt our assertion that children love sports. According to the Council's most recent yearly survey to determine the physical health of America's youth, the fitness of our youngsters has never been worse. Young Americans are increasingly inactive and ply their bodies with junk food. Unless reversed, this move away from a healthy lifestyle will have a major impact on the abilities of our young people to compete on and off the playing fields. If sports are so valuable, why aren't these boys and girls out romping on the athletic fields? You'll find the answer to this question in a variety of responses in this book, all of which, we think, will open your eyes to a new viewpoint on athletics and how your child should participate.

His courtside manner is far from courtly. Sometimes, says Veronica, rolling her eyes, he yells. "And he calls me Brace Face," she adds. But those are minor drawbacks. Without basketball and Mr. Staniecki, she says, "we'd just stay at home, looking at walls."

Or worse. Washington Heights is one of New York's most hellish neighborhoods. Police sirens and car alarms cut through the salsa music and wintry air. "You see drug deals right in front of your face, every day," says Kitty Mercado, an eighth-grader with an intense round face framed by a purple headband. There have been four police raids in her building in the past two months, she says. A few years ago, a man on crack jumped to his death from a fifth-floor window; one of Kitty's sisters saw him land.

The Positive Aspects of Youth Sports

While there are many publicized stories, and probably more unrevealed ones, on the negative influences of sports, it's important to note that stories with positive outcomes vastly outnumber those detrimental to the child. In a survey of baby boomers, 80 percent reported that the person who most positively influenced them during high school was an after-school coach. This is true whether they played sports or not; perhaps the "coach" was a voice or drama teacher, a scout leader or a youth director.

We constantly hear young people speak with respect for the coach who promotes teamwork, self-esteem, morality, positive attitudes, fairness, and who cherishes these attributes more than the win/loss record. Sports provide a unique setting for teaching these values.

Mr. Staniecki makes his kids work, and not just at basketball. Kitty Mercado and several teammates regularly cut out of practice early to help with Special Olympics, one of many service efforts Mr. Staniecki expects from his players. To support the team, the girls also hawk raffle tickets, candy, and advertising in school calendars and programs.

The team — and Mr. Staniecki — stick to a relentless schedule. He figures that the busier he keeps the girls, the better off they are. The competition and long van rides can translate into fifteen-hour days. But Mr. Staniecki says the Angels provide a respite from the suicide attempts, disintegrating families, and academic woes he must deal with at school.

Kitty Mercado's sister Sarah, a player on last year's championship team who is now in high school, says people in other neighborhoods often think that because the Angels hail from Washington Heights, "we'll come out shooting bullets instead of baskets." Mr. Staniecki tells his players that to overcome that prejudice, they must behave better than their rivals. "Street nonsense" is strictly forbidden, along with fighting, cursing, crying, or faking an injury. "They're ambassadors for the school," Mr. Staniecki explains.

Sports are fertile grounds for implanting the social values, positive characteristics, awareness and physical skills that all of us need to display throughout a long, joyous and productive life.

Philosophy of Youth Sports

A parent friend of ours said, "There are three things — not two — that you cannot escape from in the United States: death, taxes, and the influence of sports." More young people list sports superstars as their heroes than they do political, religious, educational or civil rights leaders. The average professional basketball player makes more money in a year than the President of the United States does during an entire term. While this monetary inequity seems completely out of perspective, it's a reflection of the commercial value of gifted professional athletes. Since a miniscule percentage of competitors reach sports stardom, we must look elsewhere to confirm the real value of sports:

1. Lifelong Values: Community

An elementary school teacher discovered a terrific approach to building self-esteem and leadership in her classroom and the community. She approached the local high school and asked for volunteers from the varsity football team to come to her classroom and meet one-on-one with her students. The idea was enthusiastically accepted, and a majority of the players immediately signed up to help. What started as a modest proposal rapidly grew into a weekly event during football season. The players had lunch with their young pals and invited them to come to the last game of the season as their guests. Before the game each player escorted his designated younger partner onto the field, and they all stood together for the playing of the National Anthem. Neither the players nor the elementary students will ever forget that proud moment.

Levi Strauss & Company conducted a survey of freshman high school girls and asked them who their female sports heroes were. Surprisingly, those sports figures held in esteem were not the Olympic champions or sports celebrities visible on television. To the freshman girls the athletes who excelled on high school teams were the ones most admired. It was Jade, the starting center on the basketball team; or Luke, who competed in the national ski championships. It is important to give these local heroes opportunities to pass on lessons in life they've learned on the playing field to younger community members. It's good for the givers and the receivers.

Sports are an integral part of the community and players of all ages need to be reminded that they have a civic responsibility. We have witnessed that athletic teams — given the opportunity and a slight prod — will gladly unite off the field to offer inspiration to their communities. Admired sports teams that visit elementary schools, neighborhood community groups, nursing homes, etc., can instill pride in groups and create rewarding moments for the players, coaches and parents.

2. Lifelong Values: Transforming Sports Lessons to Career Values

Investing in young people is investing in tomorrow. Forward-thinking business leaders such as Steven Covey, Tom Peters, Sally Helgeson and Dennis Waitley are among the many who have used teamwork concepts in their visions of personal success. They also emphasize the idea of value in performance as opposed to "the bottom line" philosophy of winning at any price. In both sports and career building, it is important to compete hard, compete fair, adhere to personal values, and strive for outcomes that have social merit. Sports programs with defined long-term benefits embrace these honored principles in the hope that they will dominate future decisions about business, family and community. Blending the best parts of education, sports, business and family make all four better.

A 1988 Columbia University Graduate School study (see table below) asked chief executives of America's largest corporations to list those qualifications they thought had made them successful. Then, they were asked to forecast what leadership qualities would be most important for the manager of the year 2000 and beyond. As the following chart indicates, traits which are expected to show the most dramatic changes were precisely those which are frequently cited as being developed by youth sports programs. There is a critical need for a new type of leader embodying the values listed in the study; sports as "laboratory of life" can help develop this kind of leader.

Columbia University Graduate School Study
on Forecasting Leadership Characteristics

Characteristics:	1988	2000	Change
Encouraging	70.8%	81.7%	+10.9%
Openminded	70.5%	81.0%	+10.5%
Creative	69.5%	82.5%	+13.0%
Risk-taking	63.8%	73.0%	+9.2%
Inspiring	69.5%	84.3%	+14.8%

Management Style:	1988	2000	Change
Vision of Future	76.0%	91.8%	+15.8%
Performance-Based Rewards	70.0%	83.3%	+13.3%
Focus on Training	65.5%	79.5%	+14.0%
Empathetic	65.8%	80.3%	+14.5%
Strategic Planner	74.3%	80.8%	+6.5%

Source: 21st Century Report, Reinventing the C.E.O., Korn/Ferry and Columbia University Graduate School.

The effective leader will saturate the organization with energy and inspire employees to realize their potential.

It's very significant to note that the extent to which athletes develop the valued traits is independent of the win/loss record of their team. In many cases, athletes who don't excel benefit the most. Establishment of these traits, however, is dependent upon the operating philosophy of the league and coaching staff. Seemingly, character development is less dependent upon winning games than how the game is played. Every game has a losing team, and as long as losing team members gain lifelong values, sports are not failing them.

3. Lifelong Values: Teamwork in the Workplace and in Sports

Teamwork has been the buzzword in corporate America for the last ten years. Young people who have experienced healthy competition on sports teams have a dramatic head start in understanding this business concept over those who have not competed. One of the great contributors to sports in America, Eva Auchinclos, was convinced that young females needed to learn the rules of teamwork in order to compete equally with males for jobs. As a way of providing them with this experience, she helped start the Women's Sports Foundation to promote the principle that sports can build characteristics needed to succeed in business. It was Eva's desire that women have equal business opportunity, which meant that they must prepare themselves.

The most globally recognized proponent of teamwork in business is W. Edwards Deming, who was the architect of Japan's postwar economy and an ardent critic of egocentric leaders who personally claimed credit for their company's accomplishments. Awards in his honor are annually presented to major private or publicly owned U.S. businesses which meet stringent criteria for promoting teamwork in organizations. In Deming's model, the most important ingredient of success is building the value of the worker. Trust that all workers can perform their roles correctly is essential. With this trust, corporate teams can be made up of workers whose skills complement — rather than duplicate — each other's. Many business leaders are quick to agree with Deming that if each member of the team makes constant improvement, long-term success will be achieved. Achieving teamwork is an art form which is constantly being redefined.

It is this same principle of teamwork that coaches try to instill in their players. Athletes must trust that all team members have learned the skills to perform their role well and that they are committed to the team's goals. Humility is not behind the statement of the quarterback when he says, "I only look good because the players on the line did a great job." He's not being humble; he's telling it like it is. The quarterback has to trust that every team member can do his job well; if not, he'll be looking over his shoulder at on-rushing linemen instead of downfield for an eligible pass receiver.

Deming also stressed that each member of the team should be made to feel like an integral part of the team and given a voice in deciding team strategy. NASA applied this concept to every employee, the janitor included, so that everyone believed that if he didn't do his job well, the space shuttle could not fly a successful mission.

In sports, good coaches inspire the substitutes who come in off the bench to appreciate that they are absolutely indispensible for the moments they are in the game and that the entire team, including the starters, are relying on them to do their part well.

We know a star basketball player who said to her coach, "Listen, Coach, we know they will double-team me for this crucial shot, which means Katie will be open. I know she can do it. Let her take the final shot."

Team sports thrust athletes together who have enormous differences in skill levels, life-time goals, family traditions and personalities. However, in all matters that pertain to the team, they have to work together. From this experience, young athletes learn that diversity can create stronger teams in sports and in the workplace.

Finally, Deming stressed that employees should be individually rewarded for team success and share in the corporate profits. This is a common practice in sports. When a team wins the state championships, those players who did not even play in the final game still receive a state championship trophy. The trophy helps them view them-selves as winners, and if they have the winner's self-image, they will win more often when they do play. Players on teams which do not get trophies must also feel the pleasure of being appreciated for their efforts and contributions. Positive self-image is not reserved only for trophy winners.

4. Lifelong Values: Adaptability

"You've got to think on your feet and be willing to change your game plan as you go." These words could come from a coach to the players as well as from a manager to employees. Neither author has ever coached a game or managed a situation which went entirely as planned: a key player got injured, the opposition used a strategy we didn't expect, the weather changed in the middle of the game, or any one of a thousand unexpected things happened. The same unexpected events happen in business: a competitor comes out with a new product, parts are not available when they should be, key personnel are not available, or financing has disappeared.

5. Lifelong Values: Building Strong Personal Values

"What leadership qualities do you believe players should learn from coaches?" was asked separately to 2,500 coaches, 200 sport administrators, 100 parents, and 400 players. The most-emphasized answers were similar to those reflected by the corporate CEOs' responses to the Columbia University survey on leadership qualities for the next century: positive attitude, fun, enthusiasm, teamwork, leadership, respect for others, self-esteem, risk-taking, confidence, sense of fairness, creativity, cooperation, and desire for achievement. Twelve- to nineteen-year-old players, when asked, "What qualities do you want to learn from participating on your team this season?" came up with the answers below which show that the quality of performance is more important than the desire to win above all else.

Following are their answers:

Teamwork	Fun	Contributor
Improve	Enthusiasm	Attitude
Confidence	Competitive	Self-Respect
Encourage	Perseverance	Responsibility
Acceptance	Motivation	Fairness
Discipline	Success	Respect
Skills	Humility	Participation
Friendships	Courage	Positive
Experience	Leadership	Winning
Instruction	Knowledge	Growth
Cooperation	Pride	Self-Control
Dependability	Act, not React	Commitment
Tolerance	Good Sport	Rule Follower
Assertiveness	Patience	Self-Discipline
Focus	Endurance	Goal-Oriented
Strength		

When prioritizing these values, players clearly show that fun, self-esteem, teamwork and leadership qualities are the ones most highly prized by youth.

When all the groups involved in youth sports want the same outcome, it can be (and in fact is) achieved. Study after study confirm that boys and girls do develop the traits shown on the table as a result of participating in properly run sports programs which emphasize values. The extent to which these traits are developed is the true measurement of success for a sports program. If parents, players, coaches, schools, communities and families all want to see these values instilled in youth, why are they often overlooked in the rush to win?

What Happens When Children Drop Sports?

Children don't usually drop sports, sports drop the children. This travesty should be the primary concern of all youth sport stakeholders. Consider the following consequences when high school students drop sports:

- Grade-point averages go down
- Likelihood of dropping out of school increases
- Pregnancy rates increase
- Frequency of serious injuries increases
- General health deteriorates
- Discipline fades; negative behavior changes occur

When officials of the City of Chicago announced that they were going to reduce sports opportunities as way of meeting budget cuts, concerned local business leaders, Michael Jordan among them, contributed large sums of money to re-establish these sports opportunities. They fully understood the negative impact on the community and local businesses. Young people will compete; when they don't have healthy competitive outlets, they discover harmful ways to compete.

A national athletic uniforms company, Russell Athletic, advertises: "Four out of five people in jail are high school dropouts. Some very talented athletes won't be wearing our uniforms this year." It is to everyone's interest to keep youth in school and, as you will read below, sports participation helps to do exactly that.

Keeping Children in School and Prospering

It's difficult to overstate the value of participating in school activities. The American College Testing Corporation concluded that participation in after-school activities is the only reliable correlation with success after high school graduation. Grade-point averages, college attended, rank in class, and all other student achievements were insignificant when compared to participation in some form of activity.

The National Federation of High School Associations reports that 50 percent of all students participate in extracurricular school activities. Only 2 percent of all high school dropouts come from the group that does participate in school activities, leaving 98 percent of all dropouts coming from non-participants.

As a high school principal, one of the authors discovered the "holding power" of being involved in sports activities. After many attempts at behavior modification of one student, an exit conference with the boy and his parents was held to determine if suspension or final expulsion would be the choice. During the conference the parents said, "We will do anything to keep Joe in school." With empathy, the principal stated the only way Joe could stay in school was to join and remain in an after-school sports activity.

During the next two years Joe was in his office only to receive congratulations. Through providence, the principal discovered the greatest tool at his disposal to help at-risk students. For the next eighteen years as a principal, he "sentenced" (with cheers from their parents) troubled students to a mandatory after-school sports activity of their choice. With the help of coaches and advisors, this approach produced successful students.

Sports activities not only retain students in school, they help them prosper. Studies conducted by the states of New York, Nevada, California, Kansas, Washington and Idaho all report that students in extracurricular activities achieve substantially better grades than non-participants.

Surprising to many parents, grades actually improve during the season of participation.

Parents who may be tempted to discourage their children from "violent sports contact" for fear of physical harm rest easier when they learn about sports injury statistics from Dr. Stephen Rice. Dr. Rice of the University of Washington has dedicated his career to injury treatment and prevention in young athletes. His research indicates that young athletes under proper supervision are safer playing football than riding bicycles. As a group, young people experience fewer serious injuries during an entire season of wrestling than attending the Senior Prom, and fewer injuries occur on the field or court than at home. Sports are a safe choice.

Understanding Why Young People Participate in Sports

Often parents are surprised when they learn their children's personal reasons for participating in sports. As the information below tells us, based on a Michigan State University national survey of 10,000 high school athletes, the twelve most important reasons youngsters participate in sports may be a lot different than parents imagine:

Girls	Boys
1. Have fun	1. Have fun
2. Stay in shape	2. Improve skills
3. Get exercise	3. Excitement of competition
4. Improve skills	4. Do something I'm good at
5. Do something I'm good at	5. Stay in shape
6. Be part of a team	6. Challenge of competition
7. Excitement of competition	7. Be part of a team

8. Learn new skills   8. Win
9. Team spirit   9. Higher competition level
10. Challenge of competition 10. Get exercise
11. Higher competition level 11. Learn new skills
12. Win   12. Team spirit

Two unmistakable observations can be concluded from this list. First and foremost — and confirmed by every study we have ever seen — fun is ranked among the top three reasons for a child to participate in sports. Winning has never been in the top three. Fun is true for all age groups. Whenever adults take the fun out of sports, we can expect to see a drop-out rate, and the ills of not being involved in sports will beset the child and family. Second, winning is near the bottom for boys and girls, parents and coaches. Maybe our youngsters do understand the wisdom of "play to win," but they don't want to forfeit the joy of the game. Workshop surveys conducted by the authors produce virtually the same results as the University of Michigan study.

Why Young People Quit

Four thousand boys and girls, grades seven to twelve, were asked to give the reasons why they stopped playing. Using their own words, the reasons were:
1. Lost interest
2. Not having fun
3. Took too much time
4. Coach was a poor teacher
5. Too much pressure
6. Preferred a non-sport activity
7. Tired of it

8. Needed more time to study
9. Coach played favorites
10. The sport was boring
11. Too much emphasis on winning

The message to parents, coaches and officials is to make sure that practices and games are fun, as interpreted through the eyes of the player. Especially with younger age groups, the practice has to be entertaining as well as instructional. Stand-around time at practice is a turn-off for young athletes. They come to play, and standing (or sitting on the bench) isn't playing.

Deterrents to Promoting Lifelong Values

Irrational Parents

"...don't come back; you're going to have to leave the baseball field right now. You've had three warnings and it's reached the point where I won't allow any more disruptive behavior. Two uniformed officers will escort you off the field and you will not be allowed to return whenever this team is playing a game. Your verbal attack has become so abusive that the league administrators are concerned it will lead to violence!"

The crowd who heard the words of the umpire as he ejected the quarrelsome parent from the playing field responded with a loud, approving cheer as the parent strode defiantly across the diamond bracketed by two policemen.

No, it wasn't the last game of the World Series, a high school state championship, nor the crucial ending of a tournament. It was the second game of the T-ball season for third graders who were playing on their first organized team. The parent's escalating abuse had been directed at a distressed seventeen-year-old coach who had volunteered her time to teach basic skills to an eager group of girls. The pugnacious father never got to see his daughter play again that season, and he lost irretrievable memories of his daughter experiencing the joy of playing baseball and cooperating as a team member. The loss to the player, not having her father positively involved in her activities, was more grievous.

What is it about sports that can cause otherwise-responsible adults to behave in a manner which they would be the first to condemn in another setting? How ironic that parents can loudly criticize an umpire's call: "Hey, what's the matter with you, are you blind?" when the parent is 100 feet removed from the action. And even suppose the umpire did make a mistake. What prompts parents to excoriate a sports judge for a trivial mistake, the like of which instantly would be forgiven if committed by a fellow worker?

Fortunately, irrational parents are by far in the minority. However, the actions of this limited number of parents can undermine the sports experience for all the young players and other parents. At best, their immature behavior robs children of the joy they expect to find in sport. At worst, highly impressionable young people learn that crude outbursts are acceptable and model this behavior.

Officials, coaches, players and parents must be constantly mindful that the purpose of sports is to teach the lifelong values that produce healthy, joyous citizens and healthy communities. We must emphasize how family plays a critical role in helping young people achieve the maximum benefit from sports. We also must stress the key roles played by parents, player and coach. When all the stakeholders in sports commonly agree that teaching values and enjoyment are the highest priorities of youth sports, then those irrational acts which are sparked by a "win-at-all-costs" attitude will be less frequent.

Imparting appropriate values can be the criteria used for correcting an unpleasant situation before it becomes an ugly incident. Consider the following: An angry mother stood with her hands on her hips behind the opponent's bench and glared at the coach and players of the opposing team. Her loudly mouthed negative comments about the opposing team's aggressive play and its coach's decisions were heard all over the field. Not to be outdone, the mother of a player from the other team stood up and mirrored the offensive behavior. Liz, a fourth-grade player, must have wondered why she ever thought soccer would be fun.

Excessive Pressure

Without realizing it, adults often create situations in which young athletes feel they cannot live up to the expectations placed on them. Rather than face the pressure such predicaments generate, children choose to withdraw from sports. They may feel justifiably reluctant to be caught in the middle of a conflict between their parents and the coach or, equally pressuring, they may feel incapable of performing at the competition level their parents' behavior indicates is expected from them. Children are the ones forced to make adult decisions as a result of difficult and emotionally charged situations, and most have little preparation to handle this. They have been placed in a pressure-cooker.

Parents often try to relive, or improve upon, their own sports careers through their children, as the following story explains:

Tyler was gifted with an innate ability to play football and, coming from a family of three older brothers who excelled at the game, he was expected to follow in their footsteps. Like his brothers, Tyler was talented (he was perhaps even stronger and faster) but was far more sensitive, closer to the family, more eager to please, and had a different style of learning. He was not competitive and enjoyed himself most when he was alone or talking quietly with family and friends. He was at the top of his class and considered a natural leader by his teachers.

When it came time to play for the same teams as his brothers, his father — the coach — simply signed him up with the strong assumption that he was going to be another great player...maybe the best one yet. At ages nine and ten Tyler performed better than average yet was constantly criticized for not giving 110 percent effort. Tyler's father became harder and harder on him because he never performed as outstandingly as his brothers, yet with his great size and quickness, he had all the tools to do so.

By the time Tyler was twelve, despite extra help at camps, personal instruction, and relentless pressure from his father and brothers, his schoolwork began to deteriorate. He developed an impaired self-image problem, withdrew from family activities, and definitely was not himself.

By age fifteen, he could take it no more. In what his family considered a rebellious act, he quit sports. Despite being a member of the league championship team and possessing a dressertop full of trophies, Tyler hated his childhood sports experience; it was filled with unpleasant memories.

Parents walk a fine line between encouraging their children and pressuring them. Open family communication is the only way to discover the difference. If Tyler's family had respected him as a member of the family first, and as a football player second, they could have avoided years of frustration and heartache. Open communication among coaches, players, and parents is essential to create the harmony necessary for building positive values.

Self-Imposed Pressure

Some young athletes are so obsessed with being perfect that they will avoid any public demonstration to the contrary. Such an obsession is a paralyzing pressure — the perfect athlete will never exist. Following is an anecdote which demonstrates how the urge for perfection can sway the judgment of the young.

A small-college coach was travelling throughout the Midwest looking for talented basketball players who had not yet committed to a marque basketball school. While in the barbershop of a small town, he heard about a youngster who was "the best pure shooter ever in this state." Intrigued, the coach visited the player's home and heard a ball bouncing in an oversized garage. From outside the open door, he stood silently and watched the young man shoot baskets for fifteen minutes. He had never seen anyone fire the ball so accurately and with such a repertoire of shots. He must have scored with 75 percent accuracy.

The coach excitedly rushed into the garage, intro-duced himself, and told the young man that he had never seen such a demonstration in his twenty-five years of watching basketball. "Son," he said, "with shooting skills like yours, I can't understand why I haven't heard your name before. What school do you play for?" The boy responded, "I don't play for any school; I'm not good enough. Even on my best days, I can't seem to make more than 90 percent of my shots."

Youngsters can put so much pressure on themselves to be perfect that they never give themselves credit for being great, or even good. Young athletes must be made to feel comfortable starting off as a beginner and then gradually improving. Too many are afraid to make the mistakes that are an inevitable part of the learning process. Mistakes are a part of sports: mistakes by the players, mistakes by the coaches, and mistakes by the officials. The goal is to minimize mistakes, but they will never be eliminated, just as no one will write the perfect book, play the perfect soccer game, or be the perfect teacher or boss.

The I-must-be-perfect affliction is linked to an excessive fear of failure. A stream of tears or outburst of violent words might accompany losing a game if a child thinks losing is a humiliating experience. Neither winning or losing is a bad thing; being obsessed by either can be.

We mention the above pitfalls of youth sport not because they are so prevalent, but because, once recognized, they can be dealt with in a positive manner. We hope what parents learn here will empower them with the knowledge to ensure that their children have positive sports experiences. The benefits are too great to be denied.

2

Getting Started

The Greatest Value of Sport

So much is written about how sports builds stronger bodies and minds.

Many business and political leaders insist that the most memorable lessons they learned growing up — those that helped to prepare them for leadership responsibilities — were discovered on the athletic fields. Olympic athletes, former Little Leaguers, recreational swimmers, skiers and runners have attested to the value of sports in the formation of strong character. In many cases, involvement in sports has been the influence that saved children from a life of crime.

What we are saying — and it is the underlying message of this book — is that no influence determines the future qualities of a child more than the relationships he has with parents, extended family member, and authority figures who teach basic values, morality and citizenship. It has been shown that sports appeal can be used as a catalyst to bring families closer together, and the value of using sports to connect families and society is a reasonable expectation if parents know how to understand and motivate their children.

Social studies of youth sports have clearly proven that parents of sports-involved children have a "more satisfactory" relationship with them than parents of children who do not participate in sports. This suggests that kids with good parent relationships are more likely to turn out for sports, and that sports builds better child/parent relationships, including such unmeasurable benefits as a better understanding, appreciation and affection for each other.

To further underscore the importance of sports, the second-greatest influence in the life of a young athlete, second only to parental influence, is the influence of the coaches and their assistants at all levels of play. Parents who unintentionally turn their kids over to a program, and to coaches whom they do not fully support, have disassociated themselves from key moments that will shape the future of their children.

Although children develop at their individual rates, most kids fit within the standard bell curve and adjust well to athletic programs designed for their age bracket. Spotting the youngsters outside the bell curve, and providing special assistance or reassigning them to the appropriate program, is the responsibility of both coaches and parents.

It is important for parents to understand the development and maturation of their children so they can recognize the stages of growth and the emerging sense of competitiveness that will blossom later in athletic activities. Because athletics, under proper guidance, is a "socializing and civilizing" process, children on the playing field learn early the lessons of life and the values they contain. This is why the "Team Family" concept we explore fully in this book is so important.

What follows now is a description of the stages of development through which children progress:

Birth Through Two Years Old

Between birth and the age of two, activity is the most important ingredient in a child's intellectual and physical growth. Motion, such as crawling and walking, has a wide range, depending on age and motor ability of the infant. The child is unaware of outside measurement of performance and enjoys motion for its own sake. Simply swinging feet, grabbing objects adults thought were safely out of reach, or taking possession of a sibling's treasures are actions requiring some physical dexterity and are satisfying to the child. Being accountable for these actions is generally not within the scope of children in this age group; action and motion is on the top of their list. The fun is in the doing. Those in this age group play *with* someone or something.

Three Through Six

Starting at approximately age three, and for the next four years, most children are involved in developing skills learned as toddlers: jumping, running, throwing, catching, kicking, swimming and other individual physical activities. They are often done in groups; however, the child's interest is mostly self-centered, and enjoyment comes from within. Teamwork is a concept which needs to be taught; it is not a birth trait and starts to take hold usually between the ages of four and five. Like other learned skills, it takes time to develop. Most children at this age find their greatest satisfaction through learning by trial and error, and by being in control. Those who are thought to be "ball hogs" during supervised group play are acting out their natural tendencies for their age. Since children learn by experimenting and by doing, let each one have a ball! Let everyone at this age be a star! The true value of teamwork comes later. Those in this age group just want to *play at* something.

Many studies recommend non-structured sports activity for children until the age of seven or eight with heavy emphasis on simply playing, rather than learning the particulars of sport. Taking children under seven to a tennis court to explain the intricacies of the game can turn them off, and benefits they may otherwise have gained will be lost. The majority of youngsters are more interested in how it feels when a ball bounces off a racquet or how far they can whack the ball, rather than how to either hit a cross-court shot or learn the proper grip. At this time of their lives, they should simply see the game as just another fun-filled experience. Let them enjoy the experience and they'll be more excited and interested in detail when they are ready for more sophisticated instruction.

Seven Through Ten

Many child psychologists feel that between age seven and ten, children sense competition internally. The child will think he's quicker than someone else, can swim farther, or skate better, or throw a ball harder than others. He is not consumed with the notion of needing outside confirmation of his skills to convince himself he is having fun. Many in this age group have started playing games with rules for the first time and are also learning how to function as team members. Those choosing individual sports are measuring themselves and being measured by specific accomplishments as compared to their peers. Those in this age group *start the process o*f separating play from sports.

Age groupings are obviously generalities due to differences in individual physical ability and maturity level. Some who are physically able to perform but not emotionally secure should proceed slowly before choosing a team sport at an early age. A child who appears to be blessed with above-average physical ability should not be steered automatically toward more rigorous activity, because physical maturity does not reach its maximum in a uniform manner. Young people who have seemed to escape the "two-left-feet" stage will usually not continue to outperform their peers indefinitely. In most cases, children will have to pass through the awkward stage, but not all go through it together.

Parents who have sent their young athlete to private instructors or to sports camps are often disappointed, perplexed or angry after having spent a lot of money, only to discover that their early achiever starts to look more like an average player or performer. They may have missed the fact that the early stages were not a sign of excellence as much as they may have been accelerated stages of development.

More than a few youngsters are thought to be "failures" at age nine simply because nature intervened and they are now progressing normally and no longer dominate their sport. Psychologists report numerous instances in which both adult and child see themselves as losers because the super-achiever is no longer the star she was at age five or six or seven.

Eleven Through Fourteen

Children in the eleven-through-fourteen age group normally seek persons other than family to confirm their abilities; most often this validation takes place in team sports. Those who have chosen individual sports such as running, swimming, tennis, or gymnastics have gone through the selection and classification process and are competing within their level of competence. Team players need to choose at this time between recreational and competitive sports, and there are many programs suitable for both. Boys & Girls Clubs, the "Y" associations and other nationwide organizations provide excellent opportunities for those seeking the experience of playing first and winning second. Opportunities on more competitive teams are available in most communities, and they should be scrutinized by the parents before the athlete in the family is allowed to join up. It is crucial for the youngster to have a voice in the decision, and the final choice truly should be his or hers and not an attempt by parents to relive their own lost sports glory through a son or daughter. The eleven-through-fourteen age group likes to demonstrate maturity through decision making.

At young ages, children may not verbalize well, but they still communicate. What on the surface may seem to be disinterest in contact, team or organized sports, in reality may be an "excruciating" personal reason for the lack of enthusiasm. Annette may not want to play a team sport because one of the team stars made fun of her during school. Now that may not be a good reason to most adults, but it can be an enormous deterrent if you are twelve or fourteen. Finding out the "why" about your child will help you determine a lot about "who" your child is.

In order to learn if your child is communicating her feelings effectively, it may be necessary to observe her making decisions about a variety of things. A good test could involve asking her to make choices about things not related to sports, thereby determining her ability to differentiate between benefits and the cost of benefits. One example would be asking Annette whether she would prefer to go to a movie or stay home to work on a school project which is due the next morning. Another example would be to offer her the choice between visiting a friend to play computer games, or helping out at home so you'll have time to drive her to a party late that evening. It won't take long to evaluate Annette's depth of maturity at decision making. While her choices may seem obvious — who wouldn't rather be with friends — your assignment is to judge whether or not she can weigh the benefits and costs of mature decision making and to help her make the right choice. Armed with her input, parents can reach a more-informed decision about the maturity of the child.

Fifteen to Maturity

From age fifteen to maturity, youngsters are almost totally absorbed in seeking acceptance by their peers. Usually choices have been already made and levels of sports participation have been determined by many of these adolescents. Some have been stereotyped by coaches and have to overcome misconceptions about their abilities. Some are happy with choices they made. Some are still searching. It is difficult for this group to make dramatic changes in the choice of sports activity, and many are satisfied to "go along" rather than admit to their peers or parents that they made an error in choosing one activity over another. They should be challenged and encouraged to keep looking for the activity that meets their personal needs.

Few children will elect to forgo sports activity with the opportunity for fun and organized competition, unless they feel inferior, criticized, the butt of jokes or scorn. Learn what motivates your boy or girl, giving him/her the opportunity to feel "safe" confiding in you. The sharing will help bring you together. You'll discover an interesting side effect to the sports-issue question: the convening of the family circle will provide an opportunity for idea exchange leading to closeness. From this develops strong family ties which, so often, are missing in today's rushed society.

Getting Started in Team Sports

Young people performing at the highest level of sports competition have requirements which are different from those at the recreational level because each level imposes different expectations. This is true for kids getting involved at the earliest age for competitive sports or in high school. Seeking and obtaining full agreement on the right course for the child, particularly at younger ages, cannot be overemphasized. The young people are the ones who make sacrifices exchanging playtime for sports activities. Even younger ones can provide insights into their real reasons for wanting to move to "the next level," and parents need to make time to listen. Often children are put into situations in which their failure is almost guaranteed by parental decisions made "for the sake of the child," which reflect the parents' ego rather than their offspring's intention. Children who are so pressured are the ones who will reject progressive levels of competition as soon as they have the courage to defy their parents. They often rebel by quitting sports entirely or by taking up other activities they think will help them recapture their lost childhood. As a result, they do not have the opportunity to learn from sports activities, and a valuable communications tool for the future may be lost.

It's important to note that sports is not the only way to achieve self-esteem and personal victories. There are numerous after-school and family activities which fill this need entirely for those with other interests.

It is also worth noting that there are relatively few examples of young people coerced to perform at high levels in sports or other activities who later grow to enjoy those activities which placed excessive pressure on them to excel. Starting a child at a sports level too high for his stage of maturity before a parent can trust the son/daughter's judgment, or at an age before the child is able to communicate his true feelings, is sure to lead to disappointments. Even though they may be too young to offer an in-depth analysis of what they want from life or sports (many adults and senior citizens don't have a good answer to that question either), the parents need to be able to understand how their children feel about the sacrifices they'll be asked to make. You know your child, and you are the best judge of when he or she has gained the wisdom to make the sports sacrifice decision. If in doubt, wait! Or at least seek the advice of a trusted friend, experienced coach, or teacher.

Specialization: Good or Bad?

The contemporary emphasis for an athlete to practice or compete on a year-round basis exclusively in one sport plays a major role in pressuring youngsters and parents to choose specialization even though the total sports experience can be far more beneficial than "putting all your eggs in one basket." If the player in your family really wants to play in only one sport, then explain to him what he will be missing by not learning lessons other sports and a variety of coaching styles can teach. If you and the player have a real passion for one sport, however, and it provides personal and athletic growth, then year-round specialization is a consideration for you. The key is to examine the options — not simply take the single-sport route on an emotional whim. [The pros and cons of specialization are covered in detail in Chapter Eight.]

Serious Competition: Some Thrive on It

Don't be hesitant to encourage young athletes to follow a serious competitive path if that is their nature and their choice — and you, as parent, are fully aware of the personal and financial costs. There is a price to be paid, and determined young people like Janelle often are willing to pay it.

At fourteen years old, Janelle was a promising soccer player and an even better basketball player. She was the best on each of her beginner's teams and always was given leadership roles in recognition of her natural ability to encourage and inspire others. She enjoyed competition and received excellent support and advice from her family, who encouraged her to always do her best. She decided to increase the level of competition and eventually joined more challenging teams. When she realized she was no longer the best, she knew she needed to be more determined if she were to recapture the leadership roles of earlier times. Hard work and dedication enabled her eventually to be elected captain of each team she played on, and she was selected as All-Conference in two different sports. As vice president of her school, leader in her church, coach for younger players, activist in community activities, and a 4.0 student, she had tasted success at every level. In spite of being told she was too slow, or too small, or too inexperienced, she met her personal goals.

But athletic scholarships did not automatically follow, and once again she set new goals for herself. She "walked on" (no scholarship offered) at a local college and, despite being told here was no reason for her to come back for future tryouts because there was no room for her, she persevered and finally was offered a scholarship. Janelle had reached yet another goal. The support of family and her own vision of success overrode all the roadblocks. Who would predict anything but success for her in the future?

Differentiating Parent and Child Expectations From Sports

In Chapter One, we listed what high school athletes expect to receive from sports participation. "To have fun" was rated first by 70 percent of boys and girls. In a similar survey, only 59 percent of the parents interviewed listed fun as the number one outcome they want their children to experience. It would be a good idea if you were to make a list of the sports results you want for your child and compare it with what your child wants for himself. It may be helpful if you were to make a separate list of what you expect for yourself in a sports activity context. Make certain that what you want for yourself can be reconciled with what your young athlete expects to receive from sports.

Let's look at how the difference in a player's expectations can lead to frustrations, disappointments or misunderstandings instead of the pleasant rewards everyone was expecting when the decision was made to play sports.

Tom was a naturally gifted athlete and knew he could make the varsity soccer team. It wasn't that he liked soccer so much, but his best friends played the game, and he wanted to hang out with them after school and travel to competitions. He expected friendship and group status from soccer. Tom's dad had different expectations. He was a star football player during his school days. He fondly remembered attending games with his own father, and retelling the big play during dinner. Those football victories were grand moments, and Tom's dad hoped to create similar memories through his son's soccer successes. He expected Tom to play to win, and he expected to sit in the stands, the proud father of a star athlete.

Initially, Tom's dad couldn't understand his son's unmotivated behavior. It was obvious that the boy wasn't physically training, practicing and playing up to his potential. Tom was motivated, but his motivation was for different rewards than those his father dreamed for him. Many youngsters, like Tom, recall being forced into sports to achieve goals they never wanted for themselves. A wise mom recognized the storm clouds brewing between husband and son and was able to get the issues on the Team Family agenda in time to save the season for both dad and son.

Parents and guardians must remember that they will be the mother or father of someone involved in sports only for a short time, but they will be a parent forever. So make the sports adventure a positive memory. Decisions should be made that favor lifetime family relationships.

> ## Ten Ways to Save the Day
> *Being involved in your children's' sporting life is commonly a daily involvement. To make your parenting day go smoothly, we have provided ten ideas to save time, money, energy and frustration. The ideas are placed throughout the book in appropriate areas.*
>
> ## Deliver a Positive Message to a Positive Partner
> Select someone and ask him to be your positive partner for a two-week trial. The objective is to deliver to each other, sometime each day, a verbal or written compliment. Everybody needs to give and receive "warm fuzzies" each day. The message can be as simple as "You look great today" or as complicated as organizing an appreciation day. Have an agreement to communicate only positive messages to each other! Greet each other daily.
>
> Pair up Team Family members with positive partners. Assign different days of the week for each pair to exchange positive messages. Rotate partners after three or four weeks.

Getting to Know Your Favorite Athlete

In order to help select the right sport for your child, it is important to identify your child's predominant behavior. In this respect, for the parent interested in learning how behavior is tied into choice of team or individual sport, and competitive or recreational sport, Dr. Tom Tutko can be most helpful.

Discovering the right choices will be better for your favorite athlete and takes time and preparation. Dr. Tutko, one of America's foremost sports psychologists, has developed a list of extrinsic behaviors in order to help coaches and parents better understand their players. He also has developed a list of intrinsic (emotional) behaviors of children which are useful for parents to make personality observations. Both parents and coaches should look for certain types of extrinsic and intrinsic behaviors when helping children select a sport. As discussed thoroughly in Chapter Four, the expectations of parents and coaches must be resolved with "reality" for the child, or unfair pressure can be exerted on young athletes.

The extrinsic behavior traits which indicate children are predisposed to sports are:

1. Drive (the source of motivation)
2. Determination (the strength level of motivation)
3. Dominance (the need to prove to oneself as dominant over others)
4. Assertiveness (displayed as skill, talent, and confidence to take risks)
5. Coachability (cognitive skill; the willingness to perform with maturity)

Drive

Athletes get their drive from a desire to compete and triumph over the competition, or from a desire to fulfill their individual goals, such as skill acquisition, or "to make the travelling team." In sports jargon, driven players are referred to as "real competitors." They may be characterized as "poor at practice but great on game day." "Focused" is another attribute, as is "goal achiever." The tougher the competition or goal, the more the "real competitor" enjoys it. Jen loves being the underdog and taking on a challenge which others believe is over her head. Conversely, she is hard to motivate when the competition or challenge is perceived as easy. Athletes such as this are the makers or givers of upsets.

Determination

Determination is observable at four levels: involved, committed, passionate, or addicted. Most athletes are either committed or have a passion for sports. Maybe "involved" athletes are scarcer in numbers because they are unfairly washed out of many programs which expect more of players. Involvement can be at the right level if the Team Family has made other choices and considers a minimal sports involvement as fulfilling of family values.

Addiction to sports can be either healthy or unhealthy. An unhealthy addiction might arise from an obsession for attention or desire to please. Addiction is unhealthy when the individual is out of balance and fails to meet other responsibilities due to a constant focus on sports. Such an addiction frequently leads to over-use injuries and illness due to chronic fatigue.

Dominance

As is the case with addiction, dominance is not necessarily a healthy trait. There is a slight difference between wanting to be the best you can be, and needing to be the best player on the field. Dominant players frequently display emotional outbursts when their dominance is threatened.

Assertiveness

Assertive athletes get into the action and show self-confidence. They have the skills and physical talent to play well in all situations. They are energetic but also in control of their emotions.

Coachability

Parents want to hear that their children are coachable. It means that they play by the rules, make good decisions, will sacrifice for the good of the team, and display enthusiasm for the game.

In two undeserved situations athletes can, with no discredit to themselves, be labeled "uncoachable." Children who develop slowly, though they may be perfectly normal, may not be able to perform well within their peer age group. They may not have developed the mental and physical skills necessary to compete at certain levels. In the same vein, a highly competitive youth might get misplaced in a less-challenging recreational program and display athletic behavior that is too domineering or aggressive. Young athletes must be placed in programs appropriate for them.

Young athletes must learn through good coaching what extrinsic behavior is appropriate and when to display it. While coaches urge players to be assertive and domineering during competition, parents may be displeased with being pushed into the competitive spirit of the coaching process. Team Family rewards a style of teamwork that discourages dominance. Thus, the Team Family might adopt an approach of accommodation while recognizing the exuberant aspects of competition on the playing field, or the Team Family might opt for a sports program that is more reflective of their family values.

The Intrinsic Characteristics
Developed Through Sports

Dr. Tutko advises parents to watch for sports opportunities during which intrinsic characteristics can be instilled in the young sports enthusiast. He also advises coaches to build these characteristics in their players, because they are the traits of winners in sports and in life. The sought-for intrinsic qualities which sports can nurture, and which are available at all levels of sport, are:

Trust

Trust is the foundation of teamwork. In sports, business, and families we learn to trust that our teammates will get their job done and assist us if we need it. We also learn and develop the behaviors that allow them to trust us. Without trust, every person is an island, trying to accomplish the team's mission single-handedly.

Consciousness

In sports, knowing what is going on right now is consciousness. Below the age of seven it has yet to be developed. When the ball comes your way, your mind needs to be focused on the ball, nothing else. "Being all there — wherever you are," as Olympic gold medalist Lanny Bassham told us, "is essential for high-level success." Sports teaches young people how to keep their minds on the task at hand.

Confidence

Nothing builds confidence like success. A wonderful thing about sports is that every player experiences some success (this is true in a well-coached, value-driven program). Parents and coaches must reinforce success and make sure the child also sees and remembers the success. Looking at it from another perspective, everybody fails part of the time in sports. John Stockton doesn't sink all his shots. Young athletes learn that failing does not make one a failure. If your child needs to build confidence — get him/her into the right program, inform the coach that building confidence is a goal, provide opportunities for additional practice at home, and confidence will follow the small successes he or she accomplishes.

Responsibility

Typical coach talk to a player comes across like this: "Ryan, you are responsible that no one runs the ball outside of you. You can do it." Players are responsible for executing the plays correctly, responsible for getting to practice on time, and responsible to themselves and others to do their part for the team. Being held responsible teaches responsibility.

Mental Toughness

In sports, you're going to get knocked down, physically and emotionally. The only option is to pick yourself up and face the opposition again. That is the nature of sports. As the competition gets tougher and tougher, so do the players who have been trained properly. That is true physically and mentally. Mental toughness is a learned trait which the player will be able to use as she forges her career success after high school sports are gone.

Emotional Control

It seems that we can no longer look to the professional athletes to model this trait. Too often, they make public spectacles of themselves, expecting their celebrity status to excuse their boorishness and lack of good manners. But if you watch a well-coached and well-officiated youth sports program, you will notice that the kids keep their cool under duress. Coaches and officials expect it, they model it, and they accept nothing less. Good behavior becomes ingrained through repetition. Sports requires over and over, in just the course of one game, for players to remain in control of their emotions.

A striking similarity exists between these sports-modeled traits and those identified by business executives as the ones needed by future executives. Equally true, they are also the same traits that encourage interaction between members of healthy families. At a Team Family meeting, it is easy to ask a child if he trusts his athletic teammates. The answer can lead into a discussion about how important trust is in general. It is these types of discussions, initiated through the non-threatening guise of sports, that enable parents to teach values in the home.

Level of Commitment

At the appropriate time, after the decision has been made to start a youngster in organized sports, parents will need to consider the level of the youngster's commitment. A good test for checking readiness is to ask the child what she wants to do and why she wants to do it! Simply signing up for a sport because a neighbor or a cousin is going to be involved is not the right reason, though it may be a practical choice because of self-imposed pressure to put a child into sports. Don't rush the process; there's lots of time! The right time is not a factor of age, but of readiness. Lack of preparation will contribute to problems as the child moves to the next developmental stage. Most pre-team activity of children is motion-related, or exercises consisting of play without formal instruction or pressure. At the formal team level, careful consideration must be given to: (1) the effects of stress (often self-imposed); (2) the time and money a family unit is willing to spend to give the player support; and (3) readiness of the individual to perform.

Physical and emotional readiness are major consider-ations. Some children develop more quickly than others, some are more aggressive, others are more willing to take risks. Competitiveness and an ability to take and follow instructions are additional indicators the youngster should move to more formal activity. Changes can be made later, but creating a mismatch between the maturation of the child and the level of sports proficiency required has the potential to cause rejection by the child of *all* sports involvement in the future. Those who are put in the wrong place fail to experience fun, and fun is what they want!

Competition Will Come

When parents and player decide to explore the competitive route of sports, additional questions about whose needs are going to be satisfied should be answered. "What's in it for me?" and " What price am I willing to pay?" are two key ones. Is pressure being applied on the player because everyone else seems to be doing it? Children can't be expected to know how to evaluate monetary cost but need to be made aware of the price to pay for becoming adept in competitive sports. The price includes the awkwardness of making new friends, giving up time at Nintendo, sacrificing TV programs to catch up on studies, missing relatives' birthday parties, or losing an opportunity to attend a professional or college football game. For some, the devotion required for competitive sports will be a tough choice. If choices appear to be too unsettling, the time may be too early.

Some of the better athletes don't develop until junior high and others not until high school. Some are chosen or invited to start playing on community "all-star" or "select" or "Travelling" teams. Again, success and selection of a program are a parent's choice. Just remember, before making a decision you should realize there are no assurances that: 1) the youngster will make a school team or get a scholarship by playing on one of the early-age competitive teams; or 2) the "readiness" of his physical skills and emotional maturity is adequate.

A seventh-grade boy was not chosen for his school team at a small private school and was devastated by what seemed to be the end of his "career." His parents knew he had potential and a lot of determination, so they offered him the physical and emotional support to try out again the following year. He spent hours shooting baskets and worked on his dribbling. He could always be found in the school-yard working on his game and all summer he continued to perfect his skills. He turned out that fall, was selected to play, and by the end of the year made an all-star team. Eventually, he became one of the few who got a college scholarship. Failing to make the seventh-grade team was seen as a challenge by the boy who was willing to pay the price to get accepted. Everybody knew the cost because his parents planned how they could best support him in pursuit of his dream!

It must be understood that this example represents the exception: the boy who obtained an athletic scholarship while others did not. The scholarship should not be a carrot parents hand out as the reward; the joy and satisfaction of the sport is the realistic incentive. Children should be made to understand this.

Define a Successful Season

It is particularly important that parents understand their child's definition of a successful season, and that the child also understands the parents' definition. It is okay if the definitions are different, but if they exclude each other, family conflict will be the result.

Ask your child directly, "Chris, what is a successful sports season to you?" If you don't agree, you may not be able to sway her opinion; she is entitled to that. If your idea of a successful season means changes in the child's attitudes and emotions, make sure she knows you will not be disappointed if she doesn't win or excel. It's easy for children to assume they have to win to be worthy in their parents' eyes.

Set achievable objectives which define a successful season. If you are guiding your child toward higher levels of competition, be certain your expectations match his. The only way to be certain is through two-way communication, which places value on the child's views. This communication not only enables your child to enter the right sports program, it also increases your understanding of your child which — as we said before — is one of the most important outcomes of sports.

Also, don't rush into making sports commitments any more than you would rush into any other important decision. Going too fast, too soon, can have a negative impact. Remember, a lost childhood cannot be recovered.

What Will It Cost?

While only a small percentage of youngsters will consider competing at the highest levels of individual sports, such as swimming, skating, gymnastics, etc., their aspirations closely mirror those in team sports. School-based teams also have financial costs, but they generally are much smaller because most schools pick up at least some of the fixed expenses. On all of these teams, however, there are the personal costs of admission to games for parents and family, and there are emotional costs which include missed family gatherings and the sacrifices of others in the family to give the athlete first consideration.

Costs are not to be taken lightly! For some families, the financial burden becomes too great, and youngsters play in leagues and for teams which do not create a big impact on the family budget. Parents need to be aware that there are many *excellent* sports programs which are operated for a fraction of the cost of more expensive ones and provide quality instruction. These programs may not have local, regional or national competitive emphasis, but as conveyors of the value and inspiration of sport they can more than meet expectations. Before joining a "select" or "all-star" program, evaluate all the costs. (A breakout of costs is provided in Chapter Eight.)

Fund-raising has taken a larger role in sports, both in the community-based programs and also in many school districts as funds become less available. Locating a "select" team which takes care of its obligations this way has often made the difference between parents choosing or not choosing higher levels of competition for their athlete. At costs which can easily exceed $1,500 per year for each child, expense is an issue that must be considered!

Youngsters often learn their skills on the playground or in public parks and satisfy their need to compete and succeed. Often young people, left to their own devices, who compete aggressively and learn values on their own, never receive formal coaching but still are completely satisfied with their sports activities. There is far more laughter and usually less confrontation between players in these "pick-up" situations than in formalized game and practice situations. Don't take the position that your young player won't be getting the most out of sports if you are not able to handle all the financial costs. Children, with encouragement from parents, will find ways to compete and have fun in sports, even if they can't be included in organized athletic programs. Sandlot baseball and backyard basketball are excellent character-builders, particularly if parents get involved in helping to organize informal neighborhood teams.

3

The Family as a
Working Team

————————————————————————

In the 1930s families pulled together to survive tough economic times; in the 1940s they united to support our military overseas; in the 1950s they rallied to pursue the American dream of having a good job and owning a home. In the past, a unified purpose enabled the family to work together as a team. This common bond is less apparent today.

Social critics lament that the nuclear family in America has blown apart. The average parents spend only two minutes a day engaged in one-on-one conversations with their children. Two minutes! It's rare that the whole family sits down together for dinner (forget lunch), and even rarer to have a relaxed conversation about how things are in the family.

Today's families have fewer shared interests, interests shared by all members of the family, than ever before. Kids are burying themselves in computer games, new-style math and after-school activities. At the same time, parents are busying themselves with the demands of a career and finances. Time demands and individual interests of family members seldom overlap. The American dream is increasingly hard to define and harder yet to capture. Those who have secured the good job and moved into the upscale house are not reporting that their lives are the fulfillment of a cherished dream.

What, then, does it take to live the American dream of the next century? While it is true that no two families share exactly the same dream of material acquisitions or family activities, most families, the statistics tell us, have remarkably similar happiness goals.

The dream family is one in which mutual love is not only felt but expressed; it takes vacations together and enjoys them; it experiences difficulties, but works through them together in a loving manner; it cultivates interest and respect for each other, and it shares a common purpose, which is the glue that bonds the individual members together.

The Crider family of Oakesdale, Washington, is a dream family by these standards. As you read the letters of the Crider family presented here (reprinted by permission), you will see immediately that they acknowledge sports activities as the catalyst for expressing good family relationships which have been strengthened by the values learned in athletic performance.

The authors would never suggest that families which share sports are better than the families that don't. Certainly there are many Americans who don't care about the difference between soccer, basketball or volleyball. But we do know that the traditional values of sports can be inspirational, offer moral guidance, discipline and goal achievement to all members of the family. The Criders show us how sports have contributed cohesion and unity to their family:

Cotton Crider, who is Coach Mom of the Crider family, characterized sports in her family as "the stuff that touches a mother's heart, that builds families."

Demonstrating this is Katie Crider's handwritten calligraphy poster to her younger brother:

"Dear Couzy,

"It seems like you were all freshmen...you played your hearts out, but fell short. You came back strong as sophomores, showing you could play with the best, but once again fell short of your ultimate goal. Junior year came along...seemed you were as good as gold. But then one of those nights when nothing clicks...and once again you were denied your dream. And here you are as a senior. Being a champion isn't something that happens just by chance...it takes years of preparation, countless hours of hard work, dedication and, above all, a little voice inside that says 'I think I can.' You and your teammates possess these qualities; otherwise, how would you have risen each time you have fallen and faced disappointment? You picked up the pieces and came back stronger than ever. This is it, and it is your time. Go for the Gold!"

Steve Crider wrote his son Carl the following early season letter:

"Dear Carl,

"I think this is the first time I have ever written you a letter. It is something I should have done long ago, but never got around to it.

"When I was young, I used to shoot hoops on the basket by the garage and dream about winning state championships. I would dream about games like your game against Naselle and hope that someday that dream would come true. Some night I would be playing St. Johns or Reardon. Other nights I would be playing the Cougars or Huskies. Needless to say, my dreams were never fulfilled.

"To say I am proud of you, Carl, would be an understatement. You have given me more pride, more thrills and excitement than any father has ever been given. I think the only thing greater than fulfilling your dreams is seeing your son fulfill them.

"When you go out on the floor next Friday, and again on Tuesday, remember, win or lose, whether you have the greatest game of your life, or your worst, that you have made me the luckiest and proudest dad in the world. Thank you for being my son.

"All my love,
"Dad."

Another older sister, Heidi, left a note for Carl, addressing him by his nickname, "Couz," after a loss:

"Couz,
"You 'done good' tonight! I am proud of you!
"Sometimes things like this are hard to take...but they make you better...your team will come together. Deep down in my heart I believe you will win.... Go get it because it is waiting for you!
"I love you,
"Heidi."

Stephanie sent her older brother, Carl, a copy of this "Athlete's Prayer" at the beginning of the basketball season:

> "Be with me, God, and help me win this contest of today, but let me hear with humble heart the praise people say.
>
> "Let me be perfect in any form, and let each aim be true, and let me take pride in everything I do.
>
> "But fill my soul with honesty, and listen to my prayers that every time I play the game, I play it fair and square. And every victory that I gain belongs at last to you because you gave me all the strength to see each struggle through."

On another occasion, Stephanie wrote Carl after a district tournament loss. She drew a basketball net and Carl's uniform numbers on the heading of her note.

> "Couz,
> "I know it was very tough to lose tonight. But hopefully you can get something good out of something bad. After all, it's mostly the games that you lose that make you a better player as well as a better person. You are still a winner to me no matter what. Remember that when you are down, keep dreaming and believing, then anything is possible. I love you, big brother.
> "Stephanie."

Team Family Coach, Dad Crider, wrote a note to daughter, Stephanie, near the end of her 1995 season:

> "Steph,
> "Basketball is life.

"That statement might be exaggerating the importance of the game some, but one thing is certain...your life is just beginning. For several years I've watched and waited for your game to come together, and that it has, Steph. What you do now, and what you are going to do in the days ahead will make all of your hard work worthwhile. This is one thing of which you can be certain, I am the proudest dad in the stands.

"All my love,

"Dad."

Betty Crider Hereford, Carl Crider's proud grand-mother, sent a newspaper clipping to Carl with this brief, heart-touching note:

"Dear Carl,

"I thought this an interesting and inspirational item in the paper. Good luck at the district tournament.

"With all my love,

"Your Nanny (Just do the best job you can.)"

After receiving his family's letters of love and encour-agement, Carl wrote to his little sister:

"Dear Steph,

"I'm not very good about writing you, but I am always thinking about how you are doing. Being a Crider comes with a number of expectations, but you are your own individual. Strive to meet your own indi-vidual goals, whether they be in basketball or not.

"You already know the most important thing is to 'just do the best that you can and believe in yourself.'

"I remember Katie [the older Crider sister] writing me a letter when I was a senior; at first I thought it was kind of corny, but later realized it was very true.

"I just want to encourage you to be tough (you should be because I made you play football against me all the time). Stay calm and do what you know you can do. Good luck, I wish I could be there to yell Yippee!

"Love,

"Couzy."

Another Oakesdale, Washington, player, Jeannie Roellich, received this poem from her mother, Carol Roellich, Coach Mom of Team Family Roellich, on her graduation day. Jeannie starred on the Nighthawk Basketball Team in high school and was headed to the U.S. Air Force Academy, where she would continue playing basketball as a Falcon — the name of the Academy's mascot.

From Nighthawk to Falcon

Well, you've done it, accomplished so much
In so short a time, for your young life.
I remember a gangly little girl,
All arms and legs,
And a basketball,
Spending hours in the gym
  Shooting…
  Dribbling…
  Practicing.

How far you've come, through aches and joy,
Now a fledgling nighthawk — from tiger cub.
Ready to soar ever higher, ever far,
Ever reaching toward your star.

What gift could a parent give
That could ever be appropriate
To one who has everything before her?
No worldly possession seems worthy enough
For one ready to soar to greater heights.

And so, like the hawk and falcon
Who fly so swift and proud,
Perhaps the greatest gift parents could give,
Though it aches of fondest memories and love,
Is this gift of life filled with best wishes for happiness:
    Your freedom.

May your journey be strong,
May you accomplish your goals,
And, as you soar with your wings,
May you truly "touch the face of God."

During her junior year at the Academy, Jeannie severely sprained her ankle and realized she had a high possibility of reinjury if she continued basketball during her senior year. She told us, "I decided not to play my senior year precisely because sports are so important to me. I still want to scuba dive, bike, run and do other sports — and not with a bad ankle. Most of all, sports taught me to never accept being mediocre if I could do better."

The Crider family and the Roellichs have made sports a lifelong "Team Family" affair. As they have learned, sports provides all family members with opportunities to express and practice family values.

Benefits of Sports Families

Among the benefits to the family of sports are the following:

1. Sports is, generally speaking, a true-self exposure; what you see is what you get. There is no hiding the real you from the spectators, coaches, peers and other family members. The activity strips away the veneers of self-defense, role-playing, pretending and rationalizing. Sports reveals the real you, which, being genuine, is the most likable you.

2. Sports allows us to vicariously live the experiences of another person. We truly can empathize with the "agony of defeat and ecstasy of victory" that sports provides. We know the pressure of being at bat with two outs and the tying runs on base, even though we may have never played baseball. Through this empathy, we come closer to each other — it's as if we have more in common — we are sharing life.

3. Behind every athlete, from junior recreational leagues to professional sports, there is a support staff that is an indispensable part of the successes. Sports puts people on the same team, whether as players or supporters.

4. Sports is a "safe zone" for people to speak and behave the way they really feel. It is a microcosm of real life, yet, it is still a game. Young players can talk about "what's going on in their minds" when they play sports and not feel awkward, inadequate or intimidated. They are usually not so open when

talking about "real-life" issues. As such, sports helps break down communication barriers. Intimacy means speaking with our minds and hearts, and this is so often the language of sports. The advantage to the family is that intimacy can be established in sports, and then spills over into the more sensitive areas of family life.

Save the Day

Listen to Stop and Go Signs

A message bucket labeled *Stop and Go* will provide Team Family members opportunities to communicate irritation and/or encouragement. STOP signs may request that Dad or Mom ask a coach to stop annoying behavior or they may be an acceptable way to request someone to stop "nagging." A CAUTION message sends an alert before a final decision is made — look, listen and clear the intersection. A Go sign is an opportunity to compliment and offer support.

Stop and Go Message

Date: _____ To: _____ From: _____

_____

STOP   ○ _____

CAUTION   ○ _____

GO   ○ _____

_____

_____

■ ▬ ■ ▬ ■ ▬ ■ ▬ ■ ▬ ■ ▬ ■ ▬ ■ ▬ ■ ▬ ■ ▬ ■ ▬ ■ ▬ ■ ▬

The Overextended Family

If the coaches of the "Team Family" (the parents), in conjunction with all family members, have established family values, then these values will indicate when the family is stretching itself too thin in the pursuit of individual goals. Family health practitioners advocate that the primary challenge of parents is to increase the activity of family members.

But as children and parents struggle to participate in more and more events, quantity of living begins to replace quality of living. When the family finds that it's core values are threatened, then it is time to evaluate and reorganize family members' activities.

If we have learned anything throughout our careers and in our seminars, working with hundreds of excellent coaches for youth sports, it is the observation that not one single coach we know believes that loyalty to an athletic team should ever precede allegiance to the family's core values. The intent of sports is to build strong families, not replace them.

Defining the Team Family

Does just being blood-related make a family? Does living under one roof make a family? We think not! A family is built day by day upon shared experiences, some of which are positive, and some of which are negative, but all of which are shared. Families are intertwined by the nearness of their thoughts, not just the nearness of their living space or similarity of their chromosomes.

Parents "run" families, but they should not monopolize them. Every family member is of equal importance to the family. Tanya's desire to own her own bicycle can be of equal family concern as Eric's desire to drive the family car on dates. Children have different responsibilities and privileges, but this does not make them a silent or second tier in the family. Families should be a team of people supporting each other's efforts to create the best life possible for themselves as a team.

Commitment to Family

It would insult any parent's intelligence to say that families take time, energy and shared experiences. That's obvious; nothing put in means there's nothing to take out. Through our seminars, we have coached families as much as we have coached sports teams. Sports teams set aside time to learn how to work and play together, and so must families. To expect the family to become a loyal unified unit without any "practice time" is the same as hoping to win the state championships without any preparation. It just won't happen. Yet we all know families that seem to believe they can win the game of life without any home practice time.

Establishing Family Values

Martin Luther King, Jr., Albert Einstein, Mother Teresa and Mahatma Gandhi all have a common trait other than their contribution to humankind. They have all said that they owe their successes to a clearly defined value system and adherence to those values. Team Family leaders who want to teach the principles behind success must stress that success follows from a value system. Values are learned at home, and sports is an excellent entry point for a series of family discussion about values.

When C. Everett Koop, former U.S. Surgeon General, was a mere seventy-five, he played in touch football games when his extended family got together. He was the center for both teams.

The former U.S. Surgeon General is now seventy-nine, and his football career is probably over — for lack of enough players, because the family is too scattered, he said. But Koop still thinks it's good for personal fitness and for family values when families try to be physically active.

"I don't know why they don't," Koop said, "It gives a darned good feeling."

"It beats watching television," Koop said. "Families tend to sit around the TV — there's no fellowship around a TV. They don't even talk to each other."

"On the other hand, even as little activity as going for a walk gives a family not only exercise, but time to interact with each other," Koop noted. "I think we have gotten into the habit of doing our own thing."

"Spring is a good time to start a family exercise program, because doing exercise together will have time to become a habit before cold weather returns," Koop said.

Koop's focus on families and fitness is part of his Shape Up America! campaign to fight the trend to obesity among Americans. "Very few people know that obesity is the second leading cause of preventable death," he said. Smoking, which Koop battled as surgeon general, is number one.

Source: The Associated Press

— ▪ — ▪ — ▪ — ▪ — ▪ — ▪ — ▪ — ▪ — ▪ — ▪ — ▪ — ▪ —

Recognizing that people support that which they 1) create, 2) understand, 3) have confidence in, and 4) believe will lead to improvement, then, in the spirit of Everett Koop, family leaders should create an opportune moment for the family to discuss and decide which values are important to them as a family unit. For the reasons listed above, involving the whole family in the creation of the family's value system will improve its acceptance. The family has a reduced chance of experiencing success if the guiding system — which is values — is not in place. Following are some simple steps to create a value plan for the family:

Step 1. During a Team Family meeting, review and explain a preliminary list of family values (see sample family values below). Ask what each value means to each family member.

Step 2. Ask each family member to add and explain one value to the list. Repeat this rotation until there are no additions. Now the family has a complete list of all the values that should influence the behavior of its members. (Some of the values might be combined into one, or a value positioned as a subset of a more encompassing value.)

Step 3. Using the question "What's best for our family?" as the only criteria, build family consensus as to the ranking of each value. Arrange the values in descending order of importance as determined by all family members.

Step 4. Make sure that no family member is forced to make a values compromise that can't be followed or will cause unacceptable sacrifice. If this happens, resentment will grow and eventually cause a flare-up of antagonistic emotions or behavior which violates the "acceptable" criteria for family value.

Step 5. Post the family values in a frequently visited location in the home. It's okay if non-family members see the list; outsiders know our values by our actions anyway. Just as no team (sports or business) can work effectively without all members knowing the team's goals, likewise, no family should be operating without priorities that all family members accept as valid.

Using this sheet of priority values as a guide to behavior, the Team Family leaders can recognize when sporting activities are — or are not — in sync with family objectives. If not, it is necessary to reduce the amount of time and energy expended on activities incongruent with Team Family values. Just as good coaches remove distractions for their players, family coaches must eliminate activities that distract from family growth.

Sample Team Family Values

As an exercise, you may want to rank the authors' list in descending order of importance to your family.

- To provide for the physical needs of the family.
- To ensure that family members are safe at all times.
- To consider how your actions will affect the rest of the family.
- To set aside weekly "family-only" time.
- To grow and prosper as individuals.
- To fulfill our commitments as a family and as individuals.
- To pursue our dreams.
- To communicate in an honest, caring and direct manner.
- To show interest in the important pursuits of other family members.

━ ▪ ━ ▪ ━ ▪ ━ ▪ ━ ▪ ━ ▪ ━ ▪ ━ ▪ ━ ▪ ━ ▪ ━ ▪ ━ ▪ ━ ▪ ━

Individual Sports Pursuits Can
Conflict With Family Values

It is difficult to determine when the commitment to sports has overridden allegiance to family values. Families have been known to relocate so that a gifted child can train with outstanding coaches in gymnastics or figure skating. Such a move is neither right or wrong when considered by itself; it must be considered in the context of family values.

Adherence to family norms should not fetter personal growth, nor should one family member's individual needs consume an inordinate amount of family resources. A family that knows its values and communicates openly and honestly can find the healthy balance.

Establishing Family Rules
Based on Family Values

Family values are best expressed in the truism, "Actions speak louder than words." It is not enough to just mouth our values or write them down. Yes, that's a necessary start, but values are true only when lived, when our behavior is a reflection of our values. Correct behavior is that behavior which follows the pre-established rules for the specific occasion. There are rules for etiquette, for arguing a legal case, for driving a car, and for contesting an athletic event. Life has rules, and family life will especially benefit from establishing rules.

Impress upon the young members of your family that, without rules, chaos would prevail. Young people generally want to do the right thing; the only way they can know that they behaved correctly is by adherence to the rules. Rules tell young people what is safe to do. Without rules to guide them, their experience will not allow them to act in a confident manner. It should be easy for you, the parent leader of the Team Family, to express the justification of family rules without falling back on the "because I said so" mandate.

Team Family rules, to include the unwritten ones, are established to promote the general welfare of the entire family. To be effective, parents should never agree that rules are made to be broken. When a rule is no longer relevant, or needs to be changed due to new circumstances, officially discard it rather than ignore and disobey it.

Rules in sports give kids the latitude to play the game fairly and safely. Family rules should also give them the latitude to play the game of life and grow with the freedom to make choices.

Why Kids Bend, Break or Ignore Rules

Do your children a favor: support them with some hard-and-fast rules (values) that are not up for debate or left to their discretion. From the age they understand "no" until the age of accepting responsibility, your values are your children's security blanket. Dr. Benjamin Spock would not have made a good coach because his early teaching discouraged following rules and encouraged children to make their own personal decisions.

If choices are being made by a family member to bend, break or ignore a rule, test the rule against these five criteria used by coaches of youth sports:
1. Are the rules, written and unwritten, clearly understood and does each player accept the fact that rules must be followed or the team will suffer? (All

runners on a relay team must run inside their lanes; shortcuts punish the team.)

2. Does violating the rule serve an outside-the-team value? (Talking back to a coach — or parent — may violate a "rule," but it could demonstrate independence to teammates.)

3. Is the initial reason for establishing the rule still valid? (When most of today's parents played, no water was allowed to be taken during practice. Today, dehydration is a serious health concern, and coaches schedule "must-take-water" breaks. Whether the concern is for physical or psychological safety, rules must be updated.)

4. Does the rule conflict with other rules? (A teenage son chose to miss practice to attend a special tutoring session arranged by his parents. The decision cost him a team position for the next match. He was caught between two rules: the unwritten family rule of living up to family commitments, and sports common law: "no practice, no play.")

5. Is the rule important to the rest of the team (family)? (All but six high school football team members broke training rules by attending a kegger. Some led the rule-breakers to believe "they can't kick us all off," but *they* did! The remaining games of the season were cancelled and the state association authorized the six to play for any geographically contiguous school's team, providing the host school approved.)

Sports Rules Are Effective Family Rules

If your baseball team doesn't know the rules, or can't follow the rules, it won't be a cohesive team. In both families and sport teams, there are desired outcomes/objectives which require establishing and following rules. The following family objectives and rules provide an excellent model:

Family Objective A: To build family cohesiveness by holding regular family meetings. (Wednesday evening during dinner and for one hour afterwards, for example).

Rule 1. Any family member may place an item on the agenda for discussion. The person submitting the item will introduce the topic and lead the discussion.

Rule 2. Unexcused tardiness is not acceptable; permission to miss a meeting is granted only for reasons beyond the control of the requestor.

Rule 3. No TV, phone calls, or other distractions permitted during the meeting. The sports equivalent for Objective A is: Team objectives (values) take priority over individual benefits.

Family Objective B: To acknowledge that every member has to pitch in, with both time and energy, to make the family team a success.

Rule 4. Complete assigned family responsibilities by the due date.

Rule 5. Equity of family assignments and personal contributions made will be reviewed during family meetings only

Family Objective C: To respect the needs, time requirements, and dignity of others.

Rule 6. Ask permission before borrowing equipment belonging to others.

Rule 7. Do your homework (and work from the office) during the family-established time and in the established location.

Rule 8. Notify your Team Family leader if you were asked to do something that stretches or breaks family values.

Rule 9. Do not use belittling names, even in jest, when referring to other team members.

Rule 10. If something is bothering you, express it to the family first, and include what relief/support you need.

Rule 11. Don't gripe about that which cannot be changed.

By substituting "team" for "family," especially in rules eight through eleven, it is easily seen how rules can be interchanged between sport and family. Parents can effectively model coaches and vice-versa.

Team Family Goal Setting

Clarifying values and setting rules are usually interpreted by children as setting restrictions. While it is necessary for children to have boundaries, values and rules don't excite kids to go out and achieve something important. That's where goals come in.

Goals build excitement about how we want the future to be. Families need goals as much as they need rules. Make sure that several family goals involve every family member. Talk about the family goals frequently — the target needs to always be in sight. For information on goal-setting techniques and ideas, see Chapter Eight.

Time Management in the Team Family.

All family members will benefit by organizing their day and week around both family priorities and individual priorities. These combined priorities should not consume 100 percent of the available time and energy. Time away from the family, as well as "down time" is needed to revitalize. Revitalization is the process that gives us the energy to provide quality time to family priorities rather than just token time.

Parents must be tuned into the choices and behavior of their young athletes to be sure they are not put into time-demand situations they cannot manage and which will result in burn-out. Sports is a great way to release energy and channel competitive behavior into positive and rewarding activities. Something is wrong when young athletes display the telltale signs of excessive stress: a drop in grades, poor attitude, change in physical appearance, lack of interest in friends, and altered eating habits.

As we reported earlier, the grades of most students actually go up during the in-season for their sport. One of the authors recently coached two select teams that had combined grade-point averages of 3.8 and 3.7. This would suggest that athletes have time for both sports and school-work. That's probably a fair assessment; athletes can handle two things at once. But, as we know, there are family matters, birthday parties, personal concerns, and more. Parents frequently inform us that their kids really are up against severe time constraints.

While some young athletes are over-extended in terms of available time, it is more frequent for young athletes to be over-extended with mental pressures. It takes a lot of energy to be accepted by peers at school, to figure out one's life, to worry about the big game, and the myriad of kids' concerns that we sometimes forget. Burn-out occurs when young athletes exceed their available mental energy. "Pressure management" is as important as "time management" in assuring that young people have the vitality to face daily challenges.

Recipe for Team Family Success

Start with an overabundance of love, mix in reasonable expectation, add a dash of achievement and huge portions of support. Keep "fun" always ready to pour in, spice with laughter, shared tears, and family pride. Mix in lots of patience and understanding; include only promises kept. Let simmer for about six seasons and then steep well during four years of high school. Heat only in achievable degrees of realism; do not overheat for temporary wins. Keep Cookin'.

Team Family Code of Ethics

Following is a suggested Team Family code of ethics. It is a model every family with a player in the household should consider adopting.

- Be a dependable advocate of sports integrity.
- Understand and model sportsmanship at home and at games.
- Willingly support fair play and competitive equality.
- Recognize that coaches coach teams; parents coach a family.
- Make decisions favoring performers, not performances.
- Refuse to surrender parental judgment to special interests.
- Pursue opportunities to increase all players' confidence.
- Share responsibility for Team Family decisions.
- Refer complaints to the "complainee."
- Show pride in your player, win or lose.

- Be caring, open, and honest with the entire team of which your player is a member, as well as opposing teams with whom you come in contact.
- Scoreboards do not make winners or losers; Team Family does.
- Coach Team Family with creativity, understanding, confidence, and belief in the improvement of the player and the family group support system.

Recognizing Conflict

Conflict within the family and within sports programs fall into three categories. Lack of conflict is not necessarily a measure of team success; on the other hand, dealing with conflict is crucial for success.

The first type of conflict to watch for and usually the most difficult to resolve, results when a person or team pledges loyalty to two opposing value systems. To clear this conflict, there has to be a meeting between those responsible for upholding the separate value systems. For example, John, a freshman on the JV soccer team, was encouraged to show "spirit" by vandalizing the opponent's mascot. An assistant coach was aware of the plans. John notified his dad (probably an attempt to justify saying no), and was told to "make your own decision." The opposing values between which John must choose, were family disapproval and peer acceptance. John participated in the vandalizing, admitted his involvement, and was disciplined by being benched for the next three games.

Through the act of vandalism, John increased (although only temporarily) his team acceptance quotient, but he violated his commitment to family values. John's parents immediately called a Team Family meeting —

which included two younger brothers — with the intent of eliminating the potential for serious conflict. Appreciation was expressed for John's decision to notify his dad. Dad acknowledged that he should have responded to John's inquiry for guidance with a stronger and clearer message. Dad also offered that he should have volunteered to visit the soccer coach and state the conflict of values which were enveloping John.

John acknowledged that by giving in to the peer pressure he had felt, he made the wrong decision.

The second type of conflict stems from not fulfilling the value commitments made to others. Until the others believe that the wayward behavior will cease, conflict will continue. In sports, the moment a coach notices errant behavior, he or she will point it out to the athlete in a non-threatening or non-accusatory manner.

For example, a team rule might be that if you are late to three practices, you don't play in the next game. Following a second late arrival, the coach might warn, "You know the rules; let's be on time from here on out."

As a parent, supervisor, or coach, your end result is not to punish anyone — it is to change behavior. If punishment is your best option, then use it. But always know that punishment is the means to an end.

The third type of conflict exists only in the mind of the performer. Young people frequently believe, incorrectly, that their performance is unsatisfactory — that it doesn't meet the expectations of the people they wish to impress. This inner turmoil is a heavy burden.

The symptoms of this inner conflict may be a sullen little boy or girl who, with down-turned swollen eyes, says, "I'm just not any good." Olympic gold medalist Lanny Bassham (rifle shooting) uttered these words to his dad after being hit between the eyes with a routine fly ball.

"No, son" his dad said, "you are mistaken. There is nothing wrong with you. You haven't found what you are good at yet. Keep looking."

Sports, when used correctly, is a wonderful activity for building self confidence. Praise is the key. If a young athlete does something correctly only one time out of ten, make sure he or she remembers that winning moment. If the amount of praise and compliments in this world were doubled, children would have a much better chance of growing up to be the superstars — in business, sports, civic leadership, art — that we wish them to be.

Conflict Resolution

The best solution to any problem is prevention. Good parents and coaches are proactive and attempt to foresee the situations that will lead to conflict. They enforce values and rules knowing that these are designed to prevent conflict. But it is idealistic to believe that families or sports teams can be constantly conflict free.

Conflict is like cancer: The earlier you recognize it, the easier it can be eliminated.

There are family procedures that can be used at Team Family meetings to ward off conflict before it heats up family members. Begin by reviewing last week's family priorities and "to do" list. Those that were not accomplished may indicate they were not of the same priority to all family members. Unattended priorities are going to rub someone the wrong way. Team Family leaders cannot dismiss un-heeded priorities as if they weren't important — to do so role-models a bad example.

At the end of a Team Family meeting, ask if everyone is in agreement with the upcoming priorities. Try to foresee future conflicts before they arise, and agree upon a course of action when they are unavoidable. For example, assume (this is based on an actual case) the coach has scheduled a baseball tournament during spring vacation. Parents of five senior players complain because they had arranged visits to colleges during game periods. You ask for your son to be excused to attend a family wedding and you learn that the five seniors will be allowed to miss if they could not reschedule, but the coach informs your son that he will not start the first two games if he attends the wedding.

Deciding whether your son will attend the wedding is an excellent example of a Team Family issue. The solution to the problem has less long-term value than how the decision was reached. Resolving these issues as a team builds superstar families.

Values which are passed along from mother to daughter, father to son, seem to be those which stick in the memory the longest and which become part of the fabric of our lives, as author Cliff Gillies notes:

"My father explained to me, his twelve-year-old son, the real consequences of stealing our neighbor's apples by defining conscience.

"'Your conscience is a triangular thing inside your stomach, and when you do wrong it turns round and round and hurts you very much. But if you continue to do wrong, it will keep turning until the corners wear off and it doesn't hurt you anymore. Your conscience is your best friend.'

"That Team Family Gillies value has guided me through high school, World War II, college, four children, teaching, coaching, and learning life. It is still the reason I have an apple a day. Every bite vitalizes my conscience."

Discipline

It is unrealistic to believe that all conflict can be resolved without disciplinary action. Even the best athletic teams have predetermined disciplinary actions that will be applied for rules infractions. Businesses do, and families should also.

A family of two parents, a fourteen-year-old daughter and twelve-year-old son shared with us the progressive disciplinary actions (the family called them "learning consequences") their Team Family had agreed to.

First violation: During a Team Family meeting the offending member explains the reasons for the inappropriate behavior and an action plan for correcting it. The family may: 1) challenge the reasoning and ask for further clarification; 2) accept as satisfactory the action plan (written apology, steps to avoid future repetition, retribution to offended party); 3) modify or suggest additional action to the plan; and/or 4) completely reject the reasoning and plan as invalid.

Second violation of the same rule: Same process as the first violation except that there is an added penalty from the family. The penalty is a two-game suspension from the sport or favorite activity of that season. During the two-game suspension, the parents and Team Family member will attend the events together and support the team, followed by meaningful conversation.

Third violation of the same rule: Team Family reviews the action plan and determines why it isn't working. Permanent suspension from sports or activity will be imposed until the Team Family and offending member accept a new commitment to a new action plan.

Fourth violation: Professional help for behavior modification is arranged. The family will support the recommendations of the professional and acknowledge the improvements and successes.

Team Family: Your Team for Life

As Baron Pierre de Courbertin, founder of the modern Olympic games, stated, "The most important thing is not to win, but to take part. Just as the most important thing in life is not the triumph, but the struggles. The essential thing is not to have conquered, but to have fought well."

Team Family is more than a happy slogan; it is a construct of love, discipline, goal-making and pride of performance that creates in a family of individuals a bond of understanding and trust upon which all the members of the family may depend when times are trying. In a real sense, the Team Family concept is a revitalizing of traditional cohesiveness in which Americans place their confidence, their dreams and their sense of continuity, from which lasting character is built.

4

The Youth Sports Partnership:
Parents, Players and Coaches

■ ▬ ● ▬ ● ▬ ● ▬ ● ▬ ● ▬ ● ▬ ● ▬ ● ▬ ● ▬ ● ▬ ● ▬

Synergism means that the whole is greater than the sum of the parts. When parents, coaches, and players unite and work together, they can accomplish far more for youth sports than by working separately. To facilitate this union and bring synergism to youth sports, we strongly recommend that a partnership representing these three groups — parents, players and coaches — be in place for every youth sports team.

This chapter highlights the benefits of a partnership to each partner, lists the contributions partners can bring to the relationship, and recommends a practical procedure for putting the partnership in place.

The concept of formalizing an existing relationship may be new to many coaches, but if it is suggested in the spirit of cooperation by earnest parents, the coach will most likely recognize the merit of the arrangement and embrace the idea. Coaches are typically overextended, good listeners, and interested in producing better results. This makes them ideal candidates for a partnership. Parents may find the idea of forming a partnership novel, but experienced coaches understand the need for cooperation and have learned how to channel parental assistance where it is best needed.

Partnerships Need Common Ground

The easiest partnership to maintain is one in which all partners are seeking the same goal and communicate with each other openly and often. If it can be clearly demonstrated that the individual goals of the partners can be achieved as the partnership accomplishes its major goals, the buy-in to the partnership will make sense.

Perhaps the greatest advantage of sports partnerships is the fact that the relationship promotes understanding of the partners' differing points of view. A frequently encountered example of divergent interests concerns playing time. One set of parents wants more playing time for their children, but the coach is under pressure from other parents to win more games. By giving ample playing time to less-talented players, the coach jeopardizes the performance of more gifted and perhaps harder-working children who play on a winning team. While the coach and parents may not be able to resolve their differences, the partnership gives them the structure within which to understand, and hopefully, to respect, each other's position.

A well-managed sports partnership cooperatively monitors progress and implements the philosophy, goals and purposes of the sport. When a sports program — from the vantage point of one of the partners — appears to stray from the announced pre-season understanding, corrective action can be addressed by the partnership at the incipient stage of conflict. By making these adjustments, the partners demonstrate give and take to players who learn how coaches and parents model and emphasize strong values.

Benefits to Each Partner

Below we've listed the benefits of a three-way partnership among parents, players and coaches. Each of the partners should examine the benefits to understand fully the advantages that working together can bring.

Benefits to Coach: Virtually every good coach has lamented at times, "I just wish there were more of me to go around. There are so many opportunities to help these young people, but I can't possibly be everywhere at once and still have the time to raise my own family." Coaches need help; they need volunteers to complete many important tasks that must be done but which prevent them from the primary responsibility of actually coaching children.

Partners who volunteer can organize awards banquets and transportation, collect mandatory release forms, lead fund-raising efforts, or help as their time and skills allow. Parents are invaluable as volunteers. A partnership must operate so that each member has a means of contributing to the collective goals. Given meaningful ways to contribute, parents can be a valuable resource — not a burden — to coaches. The more resources a coach has, the more successful the sport experience becomes for all involved.

Making time before the season begins to discuss goals of the sports program and the areas of responsibility for each partner is an obligation coaches should assume. It will save time and headaches as the season progresses. Coaches should accept that parents are advocates for their children's interests. Most parents see the big picture and silently toil to make the sports program better without expecting special favors for their child. They possess team spirit and fully realize that by modeling unselfish behavior they are sending the right message, not only to their child but to all the young players.

Benefits to Parents: One of the greatest rewards in life, either inside or outside of sports, is being a valued member of a productive team. Humans innately cherish productivity and success. The partnership provides parents with ownership in what can be a successful venture, both for the player and for themselves. Also by contributing to the partnership, parents are closely participating in their child's life. This builds strong family bonds. Another benefit of parents' involvement in a partnership is that their children will have many more opportunities to learn lifelong values and, of course, this should always be the primary reason for the involvement of parents and children in a sports program.

Benefits to Players: Young people report a program to be more fun when their parents are involved in a positive way and are made to feel welcome by the coach. Parents need to know how they can be positive influences and the right way to help. The partnership will help them recognize, through the eyes of their children and the coach, how they, too, can be on the team.

Parents may not realize how much teenagers prize moments when they are engaged in sincere two-way conversation with adults. If adults earnestly engage in conversation and show consideration, the teenager's self-worth increases. Sports stimulates conversations; adults need only do their part well. An effective partnership will provide young athletes what they want and deserve: a positive, worthwhile learning experience.

The ten characteristics of good partnerships shown below provide a succinct checklist for parents, players and coaches to measure their effectiveness.

Ten Characteristics of Good Partnerships

1. Sound partnerships *provide active learning* by all partners. Partners become more capable of producing the desired results from participating in the partnership. The partnership is the natural place to turn when any partner needs answers and information.
2. All partners *bring personal worth to the partnership.* Each partner has to bring something of value to the partnership. Parents bring manpower and/or financial resources; coaches supply knowledge and leadership; players bring the thrill of the sport — the reason for existence. (Actually, players can and should do more than just play the sport.)
3. *Respect each other.* Players, parents and coaches model respect for the others' contributions. No put-downs.
4. Good partnerships *provide a caring leadership.* Leadership is concerned about personal feelings as well as the essential goals of the program.
5. There is *opportunity for input.* A real opportunity must exist for each partner to make a meaningful contribution. No partner should ever have second-class status.
6. *Honesty and trust* are important in partnerships. Honesty: Partners will do what they say they will do. Trust: partners will not let you down.

7. The partnership is a *commitment to progress.* It is more than a sounding board. Without seeing progress, partners will lose interest.
8. Partnerships *provide renewal.* The partnership can adapt to accommodate growth, change, new values, and new partners.
9. *Two-way communication* is a terrific result of the partnership. Listen with empathy, then advocate your point of view.
10. *Accountability* is essential. Responsibilities have to be assigned and accepted.

If these ten characteristics are present in a partnership, pride in being a member and making a commitment to the success of the partnership will be felt. A note of caution: compliance should not be confused with acceptance — especially from young partners. Forced compliance builds a hierarchy, not a partnership. In youth sports partnerships, adults must be careful to measure progress through the eyes of the young players.

"People problems," rather than "program problems," are the perennial reasons given by coaches, parents and players for falling short of the envisioned outcome. In sports, as in life, people skills and communication skills are as important as technical skills. A partnership that is lacking in communication skills has an opening for a new member — the one who can manage communication.

In the workplace, 85 percent of the people who lose jobs do so because of poor people skills. Eighty-five percent of the sport partnership's success will also depend on people skills.

Creating Allegiance to the Partnership

Forming a partnership is half the battle; getting it to endure is the other half. Whether or not the initial energy for formalizing the partnership comes from the parents or the coach, all the participants should recognize that people will support that which they:

- create,
- understand,
- have confidence in, and
- believe to be an improvement.

Let's take a look at each one of these considerations:

Create. A variety of opportunities exists for the parents, players, and coaches to participate in the creation of the partnership. It is important that the initiating partner doesn't present the "agreements" of how the partnership will work without input from the other partners. Even if several partners favor remaining passive, coax them into the creation process. "Owners" are more inclined to do maintenance, and partnerships require maintenance.

Understand. Keep it simple. Adopt a structure and purpose that will provide several significant rewards for each partner and limit it to those. This is a short-term partnership; some problems, such as changing the rules of the sport, are not the responsibility of the player/coach/parent partnership. Rule changes and such considerations should be referred to associations of league administrators, coaches and umpires.

Those coaches who schedule periodic meetings to explain the whys and whats of the sports program report that this policy helps sustain parental support. This is especially valuable advice during a losing season. Such meetings normally end up in harmonious question-and-answer sessions. Coaches should not assume parents understand just because their children do.

Have confidence in. Before the end of the first player/parent/coach meeting in which the partnership is introduced, the partners must believe that the partnership will work. Before the meeting ends, ask the essential question: "Do we all understand our role in the partnership and do we believe that all partners can accomplish their part?"

Partnership efficacy. If the coach, parents, or players believe the partnership is just a token effort without a real cause, the partnership will be ineffective. The partnership doesn't exist to rubber-stamp the coach's "unquestionably wise decisions," nor is it the platform for parents to become sideline coaches. Both parents and coaches will have to call upon players as equal partners to speak their thoughts. Done right, the partnership meeting(s) should provide self-esteem enhancement and value lessons for the young people involved.

The First Partnership Meeting

Ideally — and there are exceptions — each youth sports season should kick off with a pre-season meeting between parents, players and coaches. Typically, the coach calls the meeting so that he/she can inform the parents about the program philosophy, logistical nuts and bolts, and goals for the upcoming season.

Midway through this meeting it would be fortunate (or, better said, wise) if either the coach or parents say, "It's obvious that if we want to make this the best experience possible for the players, we need to partner up and each take our share of the workload."

As the chart on the following page shows, there are numerous activities that can be shared by any two of the partners, and a smaller, select group of activities that is shared by all three partners. Sharing is no more important than recognizing those activities which are *not to be shared*. For example, only coaches — or a designated team captain — have the responsibility to question a referee's decision, but all three partners share in the responsibility of reducing injuries.

Parents and players need to recognize that the coach must follow given rules imposed by league officials. The coach may not have the authority to honor a request to increase the team size from twelve to thirteen players. In another case, he may have signed a job agreement stipulating that he will report all instances of alcohol consumption by players to the league. Coaches have extensive authority, and they need it to do their job well, but they do not have total authority. Coaches are accountable to parents, players and league (or school) officials. Coaches need to know what rules and regulations must be enforced and then let parents and players know how these rules will affect each partner.

As a starting place for you to form your partnership, the suggested responsibilities of each partner are delineated below. You might have good reason to move one or more of the tasks to another partner's area of responsibility, depending on the needs of the group, commitment level of each person, individual talents, and team goals.

Following are areas of expertise normally assigned to the different partners:

Typical Delegation of Responsibilities:

Shared by All Partners

Keep fun as priority • Coordinate schedules • Model sportsmanship • Self-discipline • Promote community interests
Obtain community support • Stress educational benefits • Resolve Conflicts • Be a positive force.

Coaches
Game plan/strategy
Organizing practices
Contest transportation (school)
Safety skills
Skill development
Playing time decisions
Hear concerns/appeals
Teach the sport rules
Discipline/team rules
Team publicity
Team selection
Communication

Players
Conditioning
Conduct/attitude
Respect
Teamwork
Play fair
Punctuality
Improve skills
Social competence
110% effort
Attitude
Pride
Commitment

Parents
Finances
Physical exams
Insurance
Support coach
Advocate for child
Scholarships
Enforce citizenship
Transportation
Cooperation
Leadership
Motivation

Coaches – Players
Team morale
Team competitive goals
Mutual respect
Listening

Players – Parents
Adhering to family rules
Upholding family values
Home discipline
Being eligible

Coaches – Parents
Accident procedures • Return to play (timing of) • Program goals • Team socials • Team conduct codes

---

Save the Day

Delegate or Toss

When you get behind, change the game plan!

Review your strategic plan, *visualize* your day's activities then *delegate* that which you realistically won't get done. Share the rewards and consequences. Even if you have to inform people that their task is a low priority to you and probably won't get done, that's much better that making excuses later for failing to perform as others expected.

If you have rescheduled a task three times, toss it or return it!

What Do Good Youth Sports Partners Do?

Most partners understand the concept of marriage before they enter the partnership. Yet too many partnerships dissolve before the intended journey is completed. The breakdown frequently occurs in the manner in which partners treat each other. The following behavior mannerisms, if adopted by all partners, will help prevent a breakdown in youth sports partnerships:

1. Accept equal "ownership" of victories, defeats, and organizational strengths and weaknesses.
2. Combine resources and invest in each other's interests.
3. Seek opportunities to understand and to be understood.
4. Play by the rules of the sports and partnership.
5. Accept that each member must advocate his position, and yet...
6. Maintain unity of purpose.

7. Give recognition and praise for accomplishments.
8. Let go of a task if someone who is willing can do it better.
9. Employ the adopted vehicles to solve problems.
10. Support the decisions that do not go your way.
11. Build up other partners.

These behavior mannerisms are so important that it pays for us to look at them individually.

1. Accept ownership. It's easy for everyone to jump on the bandwagon when the team is winning. The coach is wonderful, and parents show up at more and more games. The next year the same coach may not have the same talent on the team — the star center graduated — and, although the coach is equally dedicated and talented, the team has a losing record. We have often seen "parent talk" change in this situation. The coach didn't regress, yet many of his/her decisions are doubted. Even the comments to players change: "Why didn't you try harder?"

It is precisely during the losing seasons that the coach and players need more support. Players need to be praised for what they did right, for improvements, not chastised for losing. Don't look for excuses for poor performance — it's possible that your team's talent level is simply not as strongly developed as other teams.

2. Combine resources. Many parents are reluctant to deal face to face with the coach, fearing consequences to their young player or their own inadequacy in discussing sports. (Very infrequently have we ever heard of a coach discriminating against a player because of his parents' behavior.) These parents either passively endure this dilemma or take their case to other parents and criticize the entire program. Following good partnership rules, they should contact the one with the proper authority to hear their grievance; this is usually the coach. Most coaches welcome constructive suggestions.

3. Share information and be proactive. Avoid the trap of spending more time seeking reasons for why things are going wrong than in solving the problem. Coaches, parents and players need to share information openly and thwart conflicts rather than place blame. If parents are out of the information loop, either because they aren't proactive or because the coach isn't a communicator, it's easy for them to doubt the coach's and players' decisions.

4. Play by the rules. Anyone advocating that the rules "can be bent for just this special incident" not only sets a bad example for youth but sends the message to the partnership that rules only apply when "they benefit me." There are rules in life, and the example of following the rules in sports, teaches this important lesson.

Players learn that if they break one of the rules of the sport, whether accidentally or intentionally, they are subject to a penalty from the referee. Parents and coaches can use this example effectively to explain to young people that there are consequences to be paid whether a team, family, or legal rule is violated.

5. Understanding the advocate's role. An important parental role in the partnership is advocating specifically for their family player, and also all the players. In this role, they are frequently advocating family values be incorporated into the sports program's goals.

Advocates need to prepare before they can be effective. Successful advocates gather pertinent information, understand the basics about the sport and program, and recommend a solution. They will be judged critically if they fail to prepare. However, demanding or threatening accomplishes little because other partners are forced into a defensive position. Advocates must also recognize what they have the ability to change and should not be consumed by things they cannot change.

The concerned partner needs to define what the problem is and deal openly and honestly with the persons who can make the change. If meetings are conducted in this manner, differing opinions can be brought to light and evaluated with all the information present. If major differences are never discussed with an attempt at resolution, then partners should ask themselves a higher order of questions:

Do I want my player to continue on this team? Who has influence over this problem, and how can I approach them for guidance or assistance? What values can I teach my youngster from this situation? Where are the positives in this, and how can I more clearly define them to player and coach? Is there a better model of communication that we can use?

6. Maintain unity of purpose. Values clarification for the sports program is an important agenda item for the first partnership meeting. Spend extra time, if needed, to be sure that all attendees know, without question, the values that will guide the program. The fortunes of the season should not prompt a change in values. If the team got off to a good start using the all-teammates-will-play value, coaches should not change policy — when facing a tougher opponent — to maintain the winning streak.

7. Give recognition and praise for accomplishments. Ideally, a young player's six most frequently expressed words should be "Thanks, Coach," "Thanks, Mom," Thanks, Dad." It is amazing what people will go through just to hear a word of thanks. Lives have been risked just for this word. If you don't see the other partners often, send a written note of thanks. Praise shapes behavior more than any tool coaches or parents possess.

8. Be willing to let go. Parents, you can't play coach or be the coach during games. You are the Team Family coach and the player advocate. A partnership requires trust: trust the coach to do his/her part. One thing you can do regardless of your team's record: cheer positively for your player, team and coach. Negativism will hurt more than help performance.

Coaches, it might be rewarding to organize the post-season awards banquet, but parents can do it just as well as you can.

9. Adopt a plan to resolve disagreements. At the first parent/coach/player meeting, the method for resolving problems should be determined. Coaches have their own preferences, but one that works is for the coach to announce: "Parents, if you have a problem, recommendation, or compliment, please contact me or my assistant first. If you are not satisfied with the results, I'll provide the name or phone number for the next-higher authority. Players, if you have a problem, suggestion or compliment, you may contact me or your parents, whomever is more comfortable to you. Now, if I have a problem, suggestion or compliment, I will go directly to the other person or persons involved. I am very approachable and know that some issues will come up that we have to resolve jointly; they always do. I prefer that you call me so that we can schedule a telephone or in-person meeting if that is necessary."

10. Support the decisions that do not go your way. Remember, some issues are not up for discussion. The rules of the sport and the rules of the league have already been established before the first meeting of coach/player/parent, and the time to change them, with few exceptions, is at the end of the season. The existence of these and other institutionalized decision-making processes minimize decision crises, which can be disruptive during the season.

Other areas, such as goals and philosophy of the program, have room for adjustment, but they also have boundaries beyond which they cannot be amended. Don't argue for total change.

Our experience tells us that more coaches, parents and players experience satisfactory outcomes from earnest efforts to correct a problem than they do by ignoring unacceptable outcomes. Again, open, logical and frequent communication is the key.

11. Build other partners up. Tearing partners down destroys your own partnership. Worse yet, it models negative behavior to young players. The more you build other people up, the harder they will try to match the vision you have of them.

Unwritten Expectations That
Affect the Partnership

It is important to realize that partnerships have unwritten expectations as well as those formalized responsibilities that are defined on paper. The following unwritten expectations are as likely to cause conflict in the coach/player/parent partnership as would failure to meet appointed and accepted responsibilities.

Expectations of the Coaches
1. They expect to be treated as the leader.
2. They expect their expertise will be respected.
3. They expect everyone to pull for the good of the team.

Expectations of the Parents
1. They expect the program to meet its goals.
2. They expect to be kept informed.
3. They expect the sport goals to mesh with family goals.
4. They expect the coach to model the values they want the players to learn.

Expectations of the Players
1. They expect a chance to prove themselves.
2. They expect to be part of a team.
3. They expect to have fun while learning the sport.
4. They expect to be rewarded for their efforts.
5. They expect to be treated fairly.
6. They expect the coach to be a model in all aspects of life.

Conflict Resolution Within the Partnership

If there are serious problems in a partnership, they need to be resolved quickly, or the partnership may face dissolution.

People have different ways of approaching each other and use various styles for getting their point across. Problems often arise when one person who handles conflict in one way is trying to communicate with another who has trouble dealing with that style. Knowing these approaches and selecting the appropriate one becomes the role of the parent/partner.

Some people want to win every interpersonal conflict; others seem too anxious to accept all opinions; others want to avoid conflict entirely; and a few decide not to participate in conflict resolution. Regardless of style, conflict must be mediated, *not* avoided. Recognize that people simply don't always agree.

People and their conflict styles are often categorized under the following four general headings. Know with whom you are dealing, and you'll know how to approach them.

The Competitor. Highly motivated to win at almost any cost. This style is characterized as being less concerned with compromise and more with establishing right or wrong. Outcome far outdistances process. This person often has no alternative but for one winner and one loser. There is little chance for resolution, so don't approach this type of person in a confrontive manner which will result in a "one-winner" outcome. Seek grounds for agreement.

The Hands-off Person. Low motivation to make changes, often thinks things will eventually take care of themselves. This approach is probably the least effective when dealing with a highly competitive person who may see irresolution as a form of not caring.

The Protector. Most parents take this approach, even though it may not be effective. They feel the playing field is uneven for their child because they lack detailed knowledge. Rather than cause waves, protectors give in but harbor resentment. The conflict has only the appearance of being resolved. This person should be asked: "Do you agree with the problem as I see it — can I help you fix it?"

The Collaborator. This approach is almost always the most effective when dealing with a coach or someone who may have superior knowledge of the sport but is unaware of individual concerns. Finding the right time and place to meet is crucial to success. The probability of resolution is improved with knowledge and compromise.

Choosing your appropriate style depends on the other person's style and your willingness to bring workable solutions to the problem, rather than being a protector who dumps it in the lap of the other person and expects him to solve it immediately. That approach almost always leads to failure.

Before there can be resolution, there has to be reasonable clarity of expectations and of the relief being sought. The solution may be as simple as redefining expectations, team goals, practice plans or playing time, rather than requiring a full-blown change of direction. Before moving to resolution, it's important to know that everybody is on the same page. Attacking coaches does little to confirm areas of agreement or disagreement; avoiding parents has the same result.

Set the Stage for Successful Resolution

1. Partners need to understand that conflict, by itself, is neither negative nor positive. People bring diversified backgrounds, perceptions, values and goals to the partnership; differences of opinion and desired outcomes are inevitable. From the positive viewpoint, conflict has the potential to bring new ideas, new ways of behaving, and new opportunities for personal growth. Differences of opinion are the seeds of discovery.

2. Understand that only one issue in the partnership is in conflict. There are many aspects of the partnership that are still binding. Don't let one disagreement create an all-or-nothing or us-versus-them situation.

3. Pick a time to resolve the conflict that assures the greatest chance of success for all partners. Young people learn this early in life; they know when not to ask for an exception to family policy.

4. There may be a lot of emotional energy surrounding the conflict. Leave it behind when negotiating a solution. This is not to say that emotions are not important; if you feel strongly about your position, say so. Just don't let the emotions or feelings get the upper hand when discussing issues. Know whether the conflict is a molehill or a mountain.

First: Define the Problem

1. Sometimes only one member of the partnership is experiencing a conflict of interests. The other partners, for example, either the coach or parents, perceive that they are exercising their powers appropriately and therefore no conflict exists. However, a conflict does exist in this case. Whether the authority figure is right or wrong, a conflict exists and must be acknowledged before it can be resolved.

2. Once both sides acknowledge that a conflict exists, the real issues must be defined to the satisfaction of both sides. Identifying the issues is not an assessment of right or wrong, it just establishes the ground position from which a solution is sought. Determine if the conflict requires one party to compromise on true needs — or just wants — which are less important. A conflict that initially appears to be over values may, in fact, be more about preferences and therefore easier for a give-and-take solution.

Take Steps for Finding Solutions

1. Carefully pick opening comments that are not threatening.
2. Ask what relief the other partner(s) is seeking.
3. Look at the conflict from the opposing partner's viewpoint and see if his sought-after relief is, from his view, rational. There are times when individual needs have to be sacrificed for the sake of the partnership.
4. Focus on future outcomes, not past injustices. Openly discuss all options that may alleviate the conflict.

On page 103 is our version of a suitable partnership agreement. It reflects the combined wisdom of working with coaches, parents and young people in sports for more than fifty years.

If It's Important, Put It in Writing

Before setting out the Partnership Agreement which follows, it is important to understand the value of putting the agreement in writing. Yes, it is best to put an agreement between players, parents and coaches into writing, not because you don't trust the other parties; it's simply that agreements put into writing are better remembered and more closely followed. The agreement also serves as an excellent evaluation form against which periodic reviews can be made. The prototype agreement we've provided *is not a legally binding contract* for any party; its purpose is to assure that all parties have common goals and understand the operating philosophy to achieve these goals.

Because there can be significant differences between the team goals and needs of recreational and high school teams, every partnership agreement should be individually tailored. Even from one year to the next, the agreement may need to be amended as the players, talent, parent input, and aspirations change.

Volunteer coaches often ask why they should take time to do all this extra paperwork, particularly since they already are spending so much of their own time at practice and games. The answer lies in an evaluation of how much not having an agreement costs them in lost practice time; dealings with parents who question treatment of their child, player attitude and skill development; and second-guessing themselves. Once they consider the total picture, most coaches will adopt some type of agreement.

Contracting for Success:
A Partnership Agreement

Purpose:

To create a positive learning environment for all team members and to develop a spirit of teamwork and self-improvement.

Expectations of Players:

Each player will be committed to making the _____ team an important extracurricular priority. Players will arrive early for practices and be ready to start playing at the scheduled time. Stretching and getting into proper practice attire will be completed before the scheduled time. Players will arrive at games _____ minutes prior to starting time. Each player will be expected to display good sportsmanship and a cooperative attitude during all practices and games. Exhibitions of "an attitude," "talking trash" or "put-downs" of teammates represent unacceptable behavior and will be considered grounds for disciplinary action. There will be clear communication between parent, player, and coaches as to definition of these behaviors. Players will be expected to "practice away from practice" to help them develop the skill level needed to contribute to the team's success.

Expectations from the Program and Coaches:

1. To provide a safe, positive and constructive environment at practice and games.
2. To treat each player as a valued individual.
3. To promote the concept that sports are fun.
4. To support teamwork and challenge players to develop and contribute their talent in an unselfish manner.
5. To reward the "little things" which are critical to success, not only the more obvious contributions such as scoring.
6. To provide competent, consistent and goal-oriented coaching.
7. To give each player a list of individual skills he or she needs to develop and work on away from scheduled practice and an opportunity to have these skills evaluated during practice.
8. To create an atmosphere where self-improvement is rewarded.
9. To provide a setting where players will feel comfortable expressing their opinions without fear of reprisal. The time and place for this exchange will be clearly defined.
10. To be reasonable in expectations of individual players.

Expectations of Parent/Guardian:

1. To emphasize the need for players to establish individual goals that coincide with team goals and the importance these will play not only during the season but also during life experiences.

2. To encourage players to be on time and ready to play/practice.
3. To stress the need for maintaining or improving the player's academic achievement during the season.
4. To review the player's "to-do" list of skill work and its accomplishments.
5. To volunteer for the many behind-the-scenes assistance coaching requires.
6. To participate at one "adult-only" practice where strategy, plays, "to-do" list, role-modeling, drills, etc., will be discussed. Put emphasis on attending all parent meetings.
7. To create a positive atmosphere for your players and their teammates. Energy spent on positive rather than negative input is a key to success.
8. To make this a successful, pleasant, and fun-filled experience.

PLAYER:

_____

COACH:

_____

PARENT/GUARDIAN:

_____

5

Discovering What Good Coaches Do

The Influence of the Coach

High school graduates report that more than any single influence during their childhood — except for their parents — activities coaches were responsible for the formation of their character. Whether coaching a school drama, student publication, music production, student government, or academic club, this statement was true. Coaches, by role modeling respected behavior, have an influence that transcends sports. Nothing could underscore more forcibly our belief that most coaches are doing an incredible job raising the children they are supervising in an activity program.

One of the reasons coaches wield such influence is that they actually spend more time with young people than many parents do. Children often report that they like their coach so much because, "He was there when I most needed an adult to talk with."

Coaches also gain influence because they are present during many of the major lessons of life which children learn through sports. In their typical concerned but objective manner, coaches help youngsters through their most difficult decision-making moments.

Most Coaches are Dedicated to Serving Youth

Most coaches in youth sports are extremely concerned about the personal growth and welfare of their young athletes. They frequently miss dinner because a troubled athlete intentionally gave the coach an opportunity to ask, "How are things going outside of sports?"

By asking, the coach knew he or she was accepting the responsibility to listen to the whole story and suggest an outcome that may alleviate a young person's concern or provide a solution to a knotty problem. Such consultations happen all the time to coaches. Many of them prize the moments when they were able to steer a troubled youngster on a solid path as the most rewarding ones in their lives.

Steve Wilson came to the United States from England at age sixteen to try a new life. His education had not prepared him for any work other than jobs at the bottom of the ladder. But Steve remembered the inspiring words from his soccer coach in England, who had told him: "Don't ever quit educating yourself, and keep believing in yourself."

It was the coach's words that echoed in Steve's mind when times got tough as he worked and studied to become a Certified Public Accountant.

Having achieved his goal and become financially successful at age forty, Steve made a trip to England for the sole purpose of "finding my coach and thanking him for the guidance that still assists me today." The old coach was hard to locate, but Steve eventually tracked the man down through the coach's brother, whom he located in a pub. At their reunion, the coach told Steve that there had never been a doubt in his mind that his former pupil would make good in America. Steve Wilson presently directs a soccer association which includes 500 coaches and believes that by encouraging coaches to provide the same lifelong values he received is one way to acknowledge the inspiration of his English soccer coach.

It is reassuring to know that your child is probably in good hands while at sports practice, but that certainly does not mean that you can disengage yourself as a parent from the child's sports experience. Whether your child is coached by a great coach, or one of the few who are inadequate and should be weeded out, the benefits to you, the family, and the athletic child will be greatly enhanced if you are an active sports parent. Remember, the coach does not know your son or daughter as well as you do, and even though he may have good intentions, your presence and encouragement may be the added factor to make the sports outcome better for your child.

Check the Coach's Education

Good coaches are made, not born. They need to know the rules and technical skills of their sport and, more important, they should possess the communication ability to impart this information to youngsters. Just knowing the sport is not enough. For a coach to be competent, ideally she should know the rudiments of child psychology, nutrition, physiology, and first-aid. This knowledge can be acquired through coaching seminars, reading and experience.

As a parent, it is completely appropriate for you to inquire tactfully about the coach's credentials. Be careful not to put the coach in a defensive position. By asking, "How did you learn the skills of coaching?" you create an atmosphere more conducive to open communication.

Experienced coaches know that their expertise is important to you, the parent, and will not be offended.

Every parent is familiar with the budget crisis in public schools. It's ironic that even though student participation in after-school activities has a higher correlation to later life success than academic standing, activities are the first to be eliminated or reduced when financial pressures are exerted. Even under normal circumstances there is very little money for a coach's education. To compound the problem, in some states without formal licensing of coaches, a teacher who has no sports training is asked to coach a team. These coaches usually do the best they can to instruct sport-specific skills and values, but the fact is they expend their foremost effort on the other classes they were hired to teach and upon which they will be professionally evaluated.

Some states report that less than 50 percent of school coaches are trained in professional teaching methods. That's quite a downward shift from ten years ago, with the result that while many coaches know the techniques of the sport, they may not understand how to teach them and how to motivate young athletes.

For the reasons mentioned, not every coach you encounter will be excellent. A practical part of all coaches' education is listening to well-intended advice from parents. Therefore, you should stay involved with your child's sports activities; ask questions of the coach, observe his behavior and the team's at practice and at games. You should recognize that it is your partnership responsibility to suggest improvements, provided your suggestions are put forward in a timely and appropriate manner. Of course, not all of your ideas will be useful; coaches usually have good reasons for their actions. Coaches know that active parents are an important factor in a successful sports program. As true as this is, it also takes a skilled coach to prevent an active, but misdirected, parent from disturbing the entire team.

Scholastic athletic associations, school athletic directors, community recreation directors and umpire associations all attempt to ensure that only qualified coaches are active in youth sports. No system is fail proof; you still must watch for inappropriate behavior of coaches who, for whatever reason, do not model the values you deem important.

It's not just "bad" coaches you must watch out for. Even the best coaches make mistakes due to judgment, time constraints or insufficient information about a particular child. Only if you are involved are you able to intercede on behalf of your child before an unpleasant incident escalates to the point where the child is permanently soured on sports.

Inappropriate Coaching Behavior

As attested by parents of youth in sports, 90 percent of all coaches do a commendable service to youth. And of that 90 percent, the majority will make good decisions 90 percent of the time. Parents, though, need to be vigilant for the infrequent moments — the 10 percent moments — when the coach or program slights their child's values or inherent rights.

A word of caution to parents: you are out of place to criticize or second-guess a strategic sports decision a coach makes without first knowing all the background. Maybe the final second play didn't work and seemed like a stupid call to you, but you are not privy to what the team has been practicing or what the players themselves recommended in the huddle. There is only one basketball and five players; the coach can't make everyone happy if three sets of parents believe their daughter should take the final shot.

Appropriate Parent Reactions

The coach of a school-based volleyball team insisted that whenever one of the players on his team hit a serve out of bounds or into the net, the player would be pulled out of the game immediately and made to do twelve pushups. These would be done in full view of fans, parents, school staff and opponents. What is the best action to take if your child were subjected to such demeaning treatment? What action would you expect the school to take?

In a case like this, a concerned parent should politely ask the coach if he or she thought such behavior was degrading. Stand your ground if the coach says no. Suggest an alternate manner of correcting missed serves. Perhaps the player could start the next practice by hitting fifty consecutive serves. Have a positive recommendation when you first confront a coach. And don't back down when it's obvious the coach's punishment is excessive or belittling to the players.

What would you do if you heard a youth program coach angrily yell at the referee: "What a stupid call! If you knew anything about soccer, you'd see that the other team has been getting away with murder and you are penalizing us for things that are not even close. I'm pulling my team off the field and will not return as long as you are the referee! You should be ashamed of yourself and your calls!"

The irate coach quoted here actually pulled her players and refused to finish the game even though she knew the referee was unlicensed, inexperienced, and only volunteered to fill in when the assigned referee did not show up. This game for eight-year-olds ended prematurely and on a negative note. What will these players remember as a result of the coach's unwarranted behavior?

Parents need to approach a coach immediately after a game when it is apparent a humiliating experience of this sort could become part of a coaching style. Outlandish behavior such as this becomes extremely difficult to correct if left unchallenged for any length of time, because silence may be taken by the coach as tacit approval. Making mistakes is integral to sports, but displays of rudeness and incivility violate rules of fair play and courtesy and should never be tolerated.

The most serious offenses, regardless of who the perpetrator is, should be reported to league officials, and the corrective action should come from them.

Behavior which is unacceptable anywhere else but in athletics should cause great concern to parents. Examples include raising the noise level to disrupt signal calling or free-throw shooting and jeering with intent to humiliate or ridicule ("You are even dumber than you look!"). Coaches who allow hurtful "trash talk" and "taunting" as a means of gaining home-court advantage send the message that winning is more important than sportsmanship. Coaches should not permit morality to be suspended during competition!

The "win-above-all" philosophy has so invaded sports at all levels that the gracious custom of the after-game handshake requires coaching and supervision. Parents of a soccer player who was struck by a player on the opposing team when he extended a hand, sued the school, coaches, state association and parents of the aggressor for damages and for negligence. In another example, the rule in wrestling which requires the wrestlers to shake hands with their opponents and their coach was opposed by many coaches. Their rationale was that the emotions of young wrestlers cannot be controlled due to the combative "nature" of the sport. In still another example, the disqualification of a Texas cross-country team for intentionally wearing shoes which did not comply with the rules was deemed "stupid" by a popular Seattle radio talk show host who based his opinion solely on a news brief he received. Jack Robert, executive director of the Michigan High School Athletic Association and former assistant director of the National Federation of State High School Associations, pleads with national audiences to recognize that "It is the sportsmanlike thing...to develop the person more than the performance."

Admirable Coaching Behavior

The authors believe that more than anyone else's, it is the obligation of coaches to curb unruly conduct from hometown fans. Sportsmanship, a commitment to ethical behavior and fair play, is learned from coaches, fellow players and parents. We have observed the effectiveness of a coach momentarily suspending play and getting on the PA system to announce, "Folks, ridiculing the opponents does not adhere to the standards we — the players and I — are trying to establish on this team. Please refrain from such action and instead direct your enthusiasm to cheering for the good plays of both teams."

Fortunately, a very important personal goal of most coaches is to assist other people in achieving those things that are important to their lives. Coaches are constantly asking their players and the students of the school to look inside themselves and find the real meaning of what they're doing.

A high school football coach was faced with a dilemma over value choices. His team qualified for the state championships and, while preparing for the game, he became aware that one of his players was ineligible, and if the word got out he would have to forfeit all his games; none of the players who worked so hard all year would enjoy the once-in-a-lifetime thrill of playing for the state championships. He knew the information was shared by only three other people and considered what really would be gained by publicizing the rule violation. The player would be embarrassed, the team denied their chance to get respect for their hard work, and the school *esprit de corps* that had rallied around the team would evaporate. The other choice — simply stated — was to cheat.

The coach made the right, difficult decision; the team did not play. As a result of his actions, he and his players received more positive recognition for their decision than if they had won the championships by sixty points.

The story was picked up by national media, and the local business community lauded the decision, as did parents and school administrators. Most coaches, when facing a similar conflict of interest, would also make the honorable and ethical decision. The eligible players in this case, though they did nothing wrong and were justifiably disappointed, came away with the biggest victory possible — a victory of personal character.

Coaches, having the best interests of the young in their hearts, create opportunities to instill lifelong values in all the young people they meet — that is the innermost reason they are coaches. During highly contested games (or at times during practice) situations arise which require the coach and players to make a values choice. The choice could involve overly aggressive behavior from the opponents, a chance to disregard the rules and not get caught, or any other example of unsportsmanlike conduct. The coach's conduct during these moments will be closely observed, and perhaps later mimicked, by the young players.

In these lesson-learning situations, it is crucial that the coach adhere to the values that promote winning in life, and not the opportune ones of the moment that might lead to a short-term victory in the game. If — during the urgency of competition — a value choice was made, that with hindsight could have been better, then during the game review coaches should discuss with players the better choice that was overlooked. Choosing lifelong values is the sign of the truly professional coach and team.

The Bothell, Washington, basketball team exemplifies how a team can promote the proper values of sports. The team presented a "good sportsmanship" award after each game to either a member of the other team, an official, or an opponent's parent who displayed outstanding sportsmanship during a game. Awards were given by a player from the Bothell team to the opposing coach, who was asked to make the presentation — an award of merit (which was given whether the Bothell team won or lost) — in front of his team. The impact of this gesture was tremendous. The true message of sports was conveyed. The after-game handshake took on a different tone and more sincere meaning. The ripple effect of such a gesture reaches far beyond those who witnessed the ceremony at the game. This is one way of returning to the real value of sports.

In the case we cited, the disappointment of losing a game may not have been lessened, but the perspective of the single loss was changed. Every coach, player, official, parent and fan who observed the magnificent gesture was positively affected and less prone to the acrimonious feelings which often mar sports. Is this a practice that you might want to start in your hometown or on your "home" team?

As a parent, do you recognize and compliment the coaches who are dedicated to teaching values to their players, including the coaches and players of the other team?

Support Your Favorite Athlete's Coach

It is in the best interest of educating youth that parents support those coaches who uphold lifelong family and professional values as the greatest rule of the game. The majority of high school coaches contend that coaching positions are usually lost or maintained based on win/loss records, not from failure to provide positive learning experiences for their players. If sensitive, value-oriented coaches are the ones you want coaching your child, be sure the authorities who hire coaches unequivocally know your viewpoint.

With this support, coaches can resist the pressure of reverting to a win-at-all-costs ethic. We should realize that if the coach is left to interpret the fans' behavior during games, it is possible for him to extrapolate that our priority is winning first, and sports values second.

Six high school coaches from a Washington state basketball league of ten schools refused to resign when requested to do so. They attributed the non-renewal of their contracts to community pressures, self-interest, failure to receive administrative support, parent interference, cultural biases, and spoiled kids. All the influences mentioned had strong voices in the requests for resignation of the coaches. The coaches claimed that the evaluation criteria given to them when they were hired was not used to measure the quality of their coaching. They believed players learned valuable life skills and that parent pressure and unrealistic expectations resulted in conflict between players, parents and coaches. These conflicts needed to be resolved by values clarification, not by coaching skills. (These conflicts should have been addressed at a pre-season partnership meeting, as advocated in Chapter Four.)

Even though public and private school policies identify values and personal development goals as reasons for offering competitive activities, few coaches believe such policies are the evaluation criteria actually used. In the competitive sports world, the most commonly applied evaluation criteria, the win/loss record, is rarely written into policy.

For many young people the best part of their day will be time spent with their team and coach. They look forward to it and should be given a safe and nurturing place to have fun and learn. Time spent locating the right coach, working with that coach as a contributing coaching staff member, and helping teach values to young athletes in the role of parent should not be taken lightly.

Responsibilities of the Coach

The following are responsibilities coaches, parents and players should understand as belonging to coaches:

Concern for safety. A primary responsibility of the coach is the physical and emotional welfare of the youth he supervises. Parents have responsibility to know how coaches will enforce safety at games and practices. Coaches have been made aware of their liability for "foreseeability" and anticipating potential danger to unsuspecting kids. Courts have ruled coaches are responsible to anticipate and correct safety hazards which might be overlooked as risks to less-experienced persons.

Teach and model values. Teaching values, we adamantly believe, is more important than teaching athletic skills. Values are what will benefit young people throughout life — not sport skills. Even eight-year-olds need be aware that coaches honor values over athletic performance or at least treat them equally. No person deserving to be called "coach" would sacrifice his players' personal values for a "win."

Role modeling is most significant when the coaches (parents too) are not acting the role, but instead are living the role. When the spotlight is brightest, when the pressure on coaches is greatest, this is the moment to display courage of character. Young people rightfully recognize that these moments expose core values of coaches and programs.

One of the authors had T-shirts made that advertised the values and skills his team embodied, such as: leadership, honesty, hard work and skills — skills such as defense, blocking out, and others. The T-shirts emphasized the importance the team placed on values as the yardstick of measuring the success of each game. By stressing values and skills equally — not winning at all costs — the author's teams have won more than 75 percent of their games over a twenty-year period. However, the victories beyond the scoreboard outweigh the 75 percent.

Develop a season-long plan. Before there is a plan, there must be a direction. Before there is a direction, the coach needs to know the wishes of players and parents, and what skill levels the coach has to work with. The plan ensures that the wishes and requirements of all the stakeholders of youth sports are considered and, as much as possible, accomplished. A plan unifies the stakeholders before the season begins.

Coaching at home, or practicing away from practice, can be just as effective as formal instruction if a plan is in place. Players must be aware of *what* specific skills need to be developed and are shown *how* they should be performed. Mental training as well as physical training follows a progressive plan. Following a plan does not exclude the most important ingredient for success in any training program: fun.

Treat each player as a valued individual. Not all youngsters are of equal ability on the playing fields, but they are of equal value as unique individuals. Coaches help young people understand that athletic performance is not a measure of self-worth. Good coaches help every young person who participates in sports feel better about himself because of the experience. Coaches must be careful in comparing one individual to another. When the coach says, "I wish you could spike as well as Becky," young people can easily come away with the impression that "I'm not as good as Becky — as a player or as a person."

Provide honest evaluations and timely praise. Proper reinforcement is one of the most effective tools in shaping behavior. All reinforcement and praise must be accurate; young people can easily spot insincere praise.

A good coach and supportive parent will accurately appraise the youngster and yet not put a lid on him. When allowed to grow and experiment, youngsters will learn how to think for themselves and be more productive individually as leaders and teammates. When flea circuses were popular, the fascination with them centered on the wonder of the idea that fleas could be trained to stay in a box when they could easily jump out of it and escape. The trick was to place a transparent lid on top of the box so that whenever a flea jumped and tried to escape, it would bump its head. Eventually, the fleas associated pain with trying to change their situation and stopped trying to do what they could naturally, even after the lid was removed.

In the same vein, coaches — through their comments — should not put an artificially low ceiling on their athletes. Nor should their praise be so excessive that the athlete is led to repeated failure by trying to reach a standard that is far beyond him. Athletes cannot be given false hope of success, but they can't be held down either. College coaches report there are many outcome-oriented players who have rarely experienced the satisfaction of being rewarded unless they were winning. They were not congratulated for their effort. Some of these young people were made to feel as if they had never satisfied anyone else's expectations and grew into insecure adults because all they heard was that someone else was always better than they were. It's not surprising to see many professional players who are now strong advocates for non-competitive sports programs at the youth level.

There are numerous opportunities for parents and coaches to accurately praise success; the success could be hard effort, emotional control, or a small step toward a big goal.

Rudy Tomjanovich, a successful professional basketball coach has been quoted as saying: "The only thing I promise a player is that I'll be honest with him. They may not agree, but they know I won't be playing games with them." Coaches who have similar beliefs will enable a youngster to develop in a positive environment.

Create opportunities for success. The reason coaches need to know the skill fundamentals of a sport and be able to teach them is so that young players can see themselves getting better, both physically and mentally, and feel successful.

Build a partnership with players and parents. (As covered in Chapter Four.)

Save the Day

Make an Appointment
Problems cannot be solved until they are understood and their causes known. Make a real or imaginary appointment with the person(s) causing the problem and/or those with authority to resolve it. With an appointment pending, you will need to prepare an explanation of the problem, the perceived causes, and the *relief being sought.* By defining the relief being sought, the problem gets communicated and you give yourself "cooling-down" time. Making an appointment saves the day and shows positive action toward problem solving.

Coaching Styles

Coaches select a style of instruction that fits their personality, the goals of the program, the players on the team, and the nature of the sport. There isn't a single best style for all situations. In general, though, coaches do, and should, remain relatively consistent within their own style of coaching. This style probably won't be the one preferred by all the parents. Many parents, still influenced by their association with previous coaches, may have a bias toward one style. Following are four descriptions of coaching styles which are commonly observed.

1. The best-friend approach. Some coaches want to be the "best friend" of the athletes they coach. There is nothing wrong with the coach befriending a player and making himself available as a listener, but crossing the line to become the player's confidante and "best friend" creates a problem. Coaches who seek popularity through a "best-friend" status often demonstrate lack of attention to the responsibilities of coaching. They fail to realize that the athletes will respect them more for the standards they set than for the temporary friendship they establish.

In defense of this style, it is true that many young athletes occasionally need a friend at sports practice more than they need instruction. They feel alone in the world, and the coach is someone they can count on. We advocate that the qualities of coaching and friendship are justifiably synonymous, but the responsibilities of coaching, from safety to discipline, extend beyond being friends.

Coaches who seem to have the most problems are those who try to "be one of the kids" and fail to establish the important separation between adult responsibilities and player responsibilities. Sports is no place for coaches to display behavior contrary to the best interests of their players.

Coaches must at all times resist the temptation to tell players/parents "what they want to hear" in order to get things done without hassle and to maintain the friendship role. Those who take this position are looking for problems down the road! The parents/players will rely on the coach to do what he said he would do. *If he can't deliver something, he should not hold out false promises.* He should always stress realism and honesty in commitment and evaluation.

2. The authoritative style of coaching ("I demand loyalty to my program") precludes young athletes from learning how to make decisions, from accepting responsibility for their actions, and from participating in the selection of the values which guide the program. Of course, there are authoritative coaches who have the best interests of the child in their heart, but who deny the child opportunities to make mistakes and grow from them. These coaches may opt for the authoritative style because they lack the communication skills necessary for the collaborative style. The authors believe that authoritative coaches with good intentions can learn a better style and become more valuable to youth sports.

If coaches adopt the "my way or the highway" approach, their ability to reach young people on their level is limited. Getting input from young people about practices, skill work, rules of conduct, and handling rule violations is worthwhile and will reduce the number of situations requiring coach-induced penalties. Young athletes can be excellent at solving or avoiding team problems — *ask them for advice!*

3. Whatever will be, will be. This approach generally does not provide players with specific direction and allows every situation the fluidity to influence the coach's decision-making. Typically, this type of leadership lacks planning and commitment. "Let's just get out there and play; whatever happens will happen," is the refrain. This is no way to run a practice, a game, a program, or a life. The *laissez-faire* style suggests to impressionable athletes that it is okay to drift through life and not take a stand on issues. Coaches who emulate this style usually do not know enough or care enough to select a more effective style.

Even if winning the game is not an important outcome, there are many times when the coach needs to guide the program and lead the players to make appropriate decisions. Practices need to be organized, techniques must be learned, and attitudes need to be shaped. The frequent opportunities to learn lifelong values in sports require an active, concerned and competent coach.

4. *Working together* (collaborators). Coaches who select the collaborative style recognize that the stakeholders in youth sports — athletes, parents, coaches, administrators, and community boosters — all have a voice in determining the direction and goals of the program. Collaborative coaches must have considerable skill; they unite the voices of all stakeholders and follow the unified path. Often this means jeopardizing a victory to accomplish another important goal of the program. Collaborative coaches encourage young athletes to express themselves and then listen earnestly to their thoughts. They do not always capitulate to athletes or parents and realize that personal growth and cohesion is built through shared decision-making.

Outcome and Performance-Based Coaching

Many coaches on all levels have a perspective on winning which places as much emphasis on *why* something happens as *what* to do and *when* to do it. These coaches recognize the difference between coaching for personal growth and for athletic performance. Outcome-based approaches are concerned mainly with accomplishing a specific objective (winning) and the success which that brings; performance coaching is centered on developing attitudes and values. Both approaches assume that proper age grouping, physical fitness levels, adequate practice time, equipment, facilities, and support are present because without these, coaches are faced with an impossible set of challenges.

Outcome-based coaching taken to its extreme is a lightning rod for coaches without any regard for the role sports play in developing lifelong values. Winning is not a four-letter word; however, its aggressive pursuit by a minority of coaches has raised questions about what purpose it serves. Emphasizing winning, or not giving proper emphasis to value building, breeds discontent in youth sports. Until the partnership determines the degree to which the program is outcome-based or performance-based, players, parents and coaches are all using different barometers for success, and frustration will prevail.

Following is a sample code of conduct for coaches:

Sample Code of Conduct for Coaches

Winning is not the only objective of my team. Focus will be on positive reinforcement of team goals and teaching young people the values to be learned from winning and losing.

I will insist on good sportsmanship by demonstrating positive support for players, parent/guardians, officials, and assistant coaches at every game, practice, or other team-related event.

I will be reasonable in my expectations of all players. Players on my team will be encouraged to place proper emphasis on school and sports and put both into perspective. Sports are an extension of the overall learning experience.

Coaching will be provided equally to all players on the team at all practices.

Player self-improvement will be rewarded.

Players and parents will be encouraged to express opinions in an appropriate tone and setting without fear of reprisal.

Parent/guardian meetings will be conducted at a time and place to be determined and as often as agreed to in the Contract (as described in Chapter Four).

Players, parent/guardians, coaches and staff will refrain from drug, alcohol, and tobacco use at team events.

A Coach's Eulogy

The following excerpt taken from an eulogy for an excellent coach seems a good way to end this chapter. It is a reminder that excellence builds a pathway to good influence that does not end.

Frank Goddard was a pioneer of the run and shoot football strategy for high schools. His successes in Florida and Washington state were measured in people skills, extending far beyond an enviable win-loss record. Frank Goddard was proud of being a coach; he made parents and players proud to be part of the team. While preparing for the next season, Coach Goddard passed away, losing a battle with cancer only his family was aware of.

The principal who knew Frank Goddard as a coach and educator spoke the sentiments of players, parents, and fellow coaches at an overflow crowd which paid their respects:

"...and he loved them all. He taught life as an act of faith. He was a bold advocate of freedom, involving elaborate teamwork and effort...he silently demanded the exercise of reason and the highest order of self-discipline...and called it "run and shoot.

Today as student athletes compete at Frank Goddard Field, they are reminded that the real victories are gained after the scoreboard lights no longer shine."

6

Selecting the Right Sport and
Level of Competition

Consider Family Activities First

Dr. Kenneth Cooper, originator of the term aerobics, asserts, "Today, medical research shows that you can exercise moderately [instead of extensively] and gain most of the same benefits as you can get from playing sports." For all age groups, it is important to keep a fitness regimen year round, and in an ideal situation family life can play a major role in meeting needs for routine exercise.

The importance of the discovery that moderate exercise is adequate, if not preferable, is especially good news for the family. Mom and Dad, who may have a physical fitness advantage over their children, can adjust their abilities to the level of younger children and increase fitness while spending family time. When exercising together, family members will experience different levels of physical exertion, yet all receive significant health benefits. Bring adventure to the family by taking a group lesson or signing up for a raft trip, horseback riding or the like. Remember, improving general health in itself is not much of a motivator for kids; let health factors be the by-product of having active fun. In addition to the benefits of physical conditioning and prevention of injury, the family that exercises together will be contributing to Team Family unity.

Maybe it's been many years since you have been physically active, and you now wear a few extra pounds. If your family isn't a family of sports aficionados, the entire family can still enjoy sports. Physical limitations can be overcome or minimized by returning to physical activity. Young people who are physically challenged have overcome seemingly impossible odds to become outstanding wrestlers, swimmers, football players, track runners, baseball players, etc. A number have achieved national recognition as pro athletes; many more have won admiration and respect of their peers, community and family with their sports performance.

Nothing turns kids on to a healthy lifestyle more than growing up in a health-conscious, active family. If parents set aside time for active playing — and genuinely show enthusiasm — kids will usually pick up the same habit for a lifetime. The gift of physical health is one of the greatest that a parent can bestow.

Athletics Beyond Family

If you and your children choose to extend your child's fitness/athletic needs beyond family activities, it is important to carefully evaluate their emotional and physical capabilities as discussed in Chapter Two. Placing children in a demanding regimen with extensive time commitments might not be the best match for high-strung youth with short attention spans. Finding a sport or level of competition more suited to their personalities will surely enhance the fun and lessons derived from sport.

Three Strategies for Selecting a Sport and Program

Selection Based on Physical Aptitude Tests

Sports skills tests measure agility, strength, speed, power, precision and endurance. Young athletes will be asked to dribble around cones, run fifty yards, throw a baseball for distance and/or accuracy, and various other tests that can be easily measured and observed. Sports camp directors and school physical education departments should be familiar with implementing these tests. Basketball camp directors should know that ten-year-olds can do well on lay-up accuracy tests but are poor free-throwers. If physical aptitude tests are used to help choose a sport for your child, be certain that only standardized ratings for the sport being considered are used.

Skills tests, according to coaches, are of value in determining which position a player is best suited for within a sport, but too often fail to predict which sport will produce the greatest likelihood of a successful experience. A factor which can make physical aptitude testing inaccurate is that as youths grow through an awkward stage, they might be judged low in coordination, when it is only a temporary stage.

Physical testing as a means of matching youth with a sport does have its advocates: For those interested in investigating sports skill tests, the authors recommend *Assessing*

Sports Skills by Bradford N. Strand and Rolayne Wilson, Human Kinetics Publishers, Champaign, Illinois.

Selection Based on Trial and Error

We believe the most practical basis for selecting a sport is to "try it," and then determine if you want to "just do it." Many youth sports have programs which expose kids to a wide variety of sporting activities, including beginners' sessions, where participating and learning about sports are the focus. The parents' role simply may be to make certain the child has given the activity a fair trial; fulfilling one season's commitment is suggested.

School sports years are divided into three seasons, so a young athlete can experience one, two or three different sports a year if they choose. There is plenty of time; neither kids nor parents should feel pressured to pick a sport early and concentrate on it. Many professional and college teams enroll their athletes in auxiliary sports with the belief that they will learn something from the "just-for-pleasure" sport that helps them in their main competitive sport. For some elite athletes, participating in a pleasure sport is their means of relaxing and recreating. If it works for them, it has relevance for broad-spectrum youth sports also.

Selection Based Upon Analysis of the Sport

You may begin your analysis of the best sport for your child by gathering information about the nature of each sport. Coaches who are active in any sport should be able to provide parents with a list of skills used by different levels of players. Coaches of team sports may have skill lists by position on the team. The questions you should ask yourself in connection with your search should include: Does the basic performance requirements and skills of each sport match your child? Other than those which every child should experience (running, throwing, catching, jumping), which basics of the sport are positive for your child? Are practices convenient? Are injuries a consideration? A youngster has to hit and be hit in football; wrestlers compete under a spotlight one-on-one; volleyball success is teamwork; cross-country runners run — forever, sometimes alone.

Selecting a sport seems like a simple process. But it can be complicated, as can be seen from the following exercise. Different family members see things from different perspectives. When asked to give their one-word impression of the key attribute for several sports, family members revealed quite diverse attitudes. This example was provided by a fourteen-year-old son, daughters twelve and ten, working mom, and former high school basketball star dad. If everyone has a different picture of the sport, then reaching consensus on the one best sport for a family member will be very difficult.

Are the attitudes of parents being copied by the son? Daughters? Do the descriptions reveal different values? Are outside-the-family influences and values being revealed? Asking the friends of family members to respond might provide interesting value comparisons.

One Family's Impressions of Sports

(Their one-word impression of each sport.)

Activity	Son	Daughter	Daughter	Mom	Dad
Football	Tough	Spirit	Exciting	Injuries	Teamwork
Cross Country	Condition	Run	Challenging	Shape	Individual
Drama	Acting	Memory	Creative	Talent	Acting
Softball	Girls' Sport	Hit-n-Run	Boring	Fun	Coordination
Hockey	Rough	Fights	Skating	Violent	Sacrifices
Golf	Fun	Walking	Mental	Safe	Challenges
Band	Music	Playing	Reading	Lifelong	Improving

Parents' Checklist for Choosing a Youth Sport or Program

Those parents desiring a thorough understanding of the sport and the organization/philosophy behind the sport will find the following list of questions helpful. Respond by circling "Yes," "No" or "Ask for more data":

1. Is the philosophy of the youth sport or program readily apparent and reflected in the team goals?

    Y N A

2. Does the coach model coaching twenty-four hours a day?

    Y N A

3. Was the previous head coach respected for the conduct of team members and coaches?

    Y N A

4. Are the costs published and reasonable for your family, with no hidden costs?

    Y N A

5. Is a list of players, parents, and scheduled meetings available?

    Y N A

6. Is a written schedule of games and practice times available?

    Y N A

7. Is game-playing time divided and equitable among players for reasons other than winning?

    Y N A

8. Are discipline procedures, appeals process, delegation of authority, parents' role in discipline decisions written and available?

    Y N A

9. Are the travel arrangements and supervision made and acceptable by written criteria?

Y N A

10. Are the notification procedures for injury, accident, emergency, or changes in routine or tradition known and satisfactory?

Y N A

11. Are the accepted reasons for excused absences, rule exceptions, and expectations of parents and boosters reasonable?

Y N A

12. Have team rules, codes, traditions, expectations been in the best interest of players?

Y N A

13. Are parents' opinions and appeals solicited and welcomed?

Y N A

14. Will my son/daughter enjoy this sport?

Y N A

15. Will my son/daughter improve skills, attitudes, self-esteem, and develop values of positive characteristics as a result of participating?

Y N A

Parents' Checklist Scoring

12 or more Yes answers: Join immediately.
10-12 Yes: Seek more information on "No" or "Ask."
9 Yes: Ask for changes to important "No" items.
8 or less Yes: Search for an alternative activity/program.

Levels of Participation: An Array of Choices

Having selected a sport, the next step is to select the appropriate level of participation. Society recognizes that sports are good for youth and an array of choices is available, one of which is likely to fit the needs of the family. Following are brief descriptions of the different levels of organized sport activities. One level is not better than the others, they are simply different in order to serve the broadest range of personal interest.

Physical education. Generally these programs offered at most schools are geared toward physical activity rather than competition. All are invited to participate. Activities are geared so that everyone benefits.

Recreational. The first level of competition is usually referred to as recreational because it is characterized by an equal-fun-and-participation-by-all attitude. Teams are chosen and official games are played, but providing every child a chance to play and equal learning opportunities is more important than the game's outcome.

These are programs offered by Boys & Girls Clubs of America, YMCA, YWCA, Parks and Recreation departments, private church-based programs, community organizations, and others. Programs generally start at age five, and some go through high school. This level of activity fulfills the needs of the greatest number of young athletes; many recreational athletes are completely satisfied to stay at this level.

Select. Select programs, as the name implies, are characterized by athletes being selected to participate rather than being open to all. Programs are offered by various national, regional or local groups, are for youngsters interested in learning more about one sport and playing on virtually year-round teams. Select team activities usually overlap other sports/school team schedules.

Select players are not more important than those at the recreation level; they've simply made a decision to become more involved. Competition skill is the dominant criterion. These talented athletes must accelerate skill development by concentrating on a single sport, or they may not be selected at team tryouts.

The select teams sports organization has its advocates and critics. A *critic* may say: The select team concept of competing at local, state, regional and national tournaments (and growing to international competitions) has the end result of catering to the elite athlete —- due to the win-or-be-eliminated philosophy. Ironically, some select programs originally organized for the recreational level have created entire leagues of children serving the "win" syndrome. For all but the talented few selected to play, this level is "no win." The league resources — physical, human and financial — are directed to the talented few: the talented rich get richer in athletic experiences, and the poor (less talented) remain poor.

An *advocate* would say that select teams can be tremendous community assets. Most are coached by people who have their own children on teams and are acutely aware of the stress families face when youngsters are playing or performing at this competitive level. While some teams play year round, others only extend a few weeks beyond the normal season. Many routinely accommodate players who miss practices or games due to family conflicts.

Don't reject the notion of your child playing on a select or elite team based on the assumption that you are committing him to unreasonable time demands. A high percentage of select players have excellent GPAs and active social lives. There are varying degrees of select competition, and one may fit your needs.

School/Competitive. These are teams which represent their schools against other schools. Rules, eligibility, coaching standards, safety and transportation are administered by state organizations, who offer championships in a wide range of activities. These are the most regulated and have the largest percentage of coaches holding degrees in teaching and/or physical education.

The school level of competition, ostensibly, promotes education as its principal purpose. However, the goal of creating a winning team introduces the concept that the better players make the team and that earning a spot on the team should be a competitive process Schools justify athletic programs as an integral part of the total education of youth, yet many school coaches ignore important principles of learning by discouraging students from receiving the education benefits that a variety of experiences (sports) and teachers (coaches) offer. In other words, many coaches stress specialization of sports — to win becomes more important than to learn.

Private Sports Academies and Instruction. Private instruction, usually but not always geared for the serious competitor, is available within a number of sports. Private coaching has become the prevailing route to the top in such sports as gymnastics, swimming and alpine skiing.

Play for Pay. The sixth level of competitive intensity is easily identified by play for external monetary rewards. In professional sports, the compensation is salaries; in amateur youth sports the different types of compensation continue to increase beyond scholarships, special treatment, travel expenses, and valuable awards. Private schools have been known to waive registration fees for selected athletes; Little

League parents report inducements for their family player to transfer to teams that are winners. The play-for-pay pressure can be extreme and, in some cases, it is justifiable and must be dealt with. For example, in certain families, the best chance to attend college rides on the hope of earning a scholarship. Those relying on scholarships need to realize that it's a long shot, and focusing only on athletics is a poor investment.

The majority of young people will choose recreational sports teams because these programs are more accessible, offer more playing time, have less stress-related competition, and because that's where most of their friends will be playing. Select players play because they enjoy the particular sport and want to spend more time in it. A recent survey of 247 players twelve to sixteen years old conducted by one of the authors showed that the qualities these "select" players expect are similar to those on recreational or school teams. The consensus report was that this level of player expected to learn from his coach the following values: fun, improvement, commitment, positive attitude, 110 percent effort. The word "win" showed up as one of the top three choices on only sixteen responses.

Individual Sports — Levels of Competition

Youngsters who get pleasure out of competing and who are willing to work on their own may discover they are best suited for participation in activities which do not require teamwork. The most common, as we have said, are swimming, skiing, running, gymnastics, skating, bowling, wrestling, tennis and golf. Parents who feel their child is suited to an individual sport also need to make selections on the appropriate level of competition. Those who choose the more competitive levels may have to pay for private instruction, and be prepared for year-round competition and training. In some sports, exceptionally talented youngsters leave home to attend schools and camps whose primary objective includes extensive personal training. Less-competitive programs often include private instruction and practice at local clubs or in school-related programs.

Individual sports provide the added benefits of lifelong participation, an advantage over team sports, which provide a limited number of activities for adults. You can play football only for so long. Those who compete exclusively in team sports will be missing out on the recreational aspects individual sports offer.

The odds of achieving professional or nationwide fame in individual sports is also formidable. Fewer than twenty gymnasts are selected for the U.S. Olympic team, yet thousands of youngsters are daily taking private or semi-private lessons. Some sports consider sixteen-year-old athletes as over the hill if their rankings decline or they fail to better rigorous standards. Is this a risk you and your son/daughter are willing to take?

Should We Specialize?

When your family is still in the process of selecting the right sport and level of competition, specialization — a commitment to just one sport — shouldn't be a consideration. Experience as many different sports as time permits.

Specialization is a very controversial topic which is usually encountered farther down the road of sports participation. [See Chapter Eight for an in-depth discussion.]

Save the Day

Jump Start Your Day:
Do the Easiest Task First

Look at your day's agenda and do the easiest task first. Cross it off when you are finished. Save another easy task for the "need-a-lift time" or to end your day with a positive result.

If you are carrying an "impossible load," unless it is an emergency you cannot postpone, take these steps: (1) interrupt or bring to closure what you are doing, (2) write down what has been done, (3) clear your working space, (4) either use a "jump start" easy task or walk ten steps v-e-r-y s-l-o-w-l-y, (5) give yourself a "fresh new start." Now tackle the impossible. Plan to be successful.

Out-of-Season Sports Teams

Sports today are divided into at least two seasons: the competition season and the developmental season. Contests are no longer limited in a sport to the normal competition (school) season; each sport, over time, has developed its own organization which extends the season start and finish. In choosing a sport, parents should inquire about any expectations your school or coach may have for extended commitment far beyond the traditional season. Year-round development is frequently the norm in competitive individual and team sports. Off-season competitions are usually limited by weather and facilities in sports such as football, for example, so there are fewer elongated seasons.

Schools accommodating both boys' and girls' soccer frequently set separate seasons for boys and girls. Even though the supply and demand for facilities has improved, the developmental season has taxed major city parks and recreation facilities. Fields are difficult to find for use by young people who simply want a place to play — not necessarily on an organized team.

Monetary Influences on Sport Selection

Sports is a good financial investment, but the return on investment rarely comes back to parents or children as a salary or endorsements by becoming a professional player. The odds of a high school football or basketball player playing professionally are astronomically slim. However, the odds of students graduating from high school increases significantly if they participate in sports. Therein lies the return on investment: lifetime earnings of high school graduates exceed by one-half-million dollars the money earned by non-graduates.

The investment of time and energy spent on sports is returned as character values and lessons in life. These are the keys that unlock the gateways to an enriched life.

Sports-minded youth who want to make sports a career should also consider coaching, sports administration, sports marketing, sports medicine, sports psychology and other fields pertaining to sports. We don't want to discourage any young boy or girl from aspiring to a dream of being a professional athlete; it is realistic, but also, to state it bluntly, unlikely. The potential of making large sums of money should not be a priority consideration in selecting a sport. (See Chapter Eight, The Cost of Playing: Money and Time, for an in-depth coverage of financial costs to participate.)

Be Aware of the Unwritten Codes
of Sports and Team

Many organized youth sports teams have a written players' code and a separate coaches' code. (If yours does not, it should.) Before signing a permission-to-play form, read the regulations that apply to all players and all coaches. Less explicit, but of equal (or greater) importance, are the unwritten codes. Unwritten codes force compliance to a standard just as the written rules do. They stem from the authority and responsibility granted or imposed upon the coach, from peer influences and from athletic traditions of the team.

The unwritten coach's code regarding emotional control is not written, but it is well understood. The values of the coach and team leaders are also reflected in the team's codes. Violation of an unwritten code is typically punished by social banishment by peers or withholding of privileges by the coach. For a youngster, this is the most dreaded consequence of misbehavior.

The written rules establish the behavior of a team, and it could be said that the unwritten rules create the personality of the team. The written rules are available for inspection, yet it is the unwritten rules that so often produce the biggest effect on the child.

Parents wanting to gauge the impact of unwritten rules can begin by reading the Coaches' Code of Conduct in Chapter Five. The following questions will help reveal how the coach and team history formulate unwritten codes.

1. Does the coach believe that behavior away from sports influences what happens in practice and competition?
2. What does the coach do to encourage leadership?
3. What are the coach's levels of discipline? Was it necessary to remove players in the past?
4. What authority to discipline has been delegated to team captains?
5. Do parents have a voice in disciplinary actions?
6. How are disciplinary violations appealed?

Rules Originally Encouraged Multiple-Sports Participation

All youth sports organizations have adopted operational rules to deal with, among other things, the inequities created by recruiting in sports. The rules, however, are designed to serve the organization, the sport, or the balance between teams. Rule violations usually punish the player rather than the coach. Historically, organization rules have served the sport or system, not necessarily the players.

When penalizing the University of Washington football program for the offense of a player accepting financial considerations provided by a source outside the school, the conference of schools penalized the Huskies football team by denying its participation in post-season bowl games for two years. The NCAA accepted the penalty as being sufficient. The system and organization was served, but it was the players who "served the sentence."

One coach has instituted a policy of allowing all his players two "free passes" which can be used as excused absences for any reason players choose. No penalties are imposed for pass use. This is an example of how coaches can make provisions to accommodate players' prioritizing of important personal needs. To nearly all coaches (and employers), absences from practices are often regarded as in indication of the level of dedication. This is not always an accurate barometer.

Beyond the intimacy of team rules, national rules are developed, adopted and administered by state associations which exist in each of the fifty states. Whether inter-scholastic or recreational, contests between teams located in different regions and states are conducted under common rules.

Strict compliance with national rules are our best assurances and measurements that the first priority is safety of players and fair play during competition. Even though excellent written and unwritten rules/codes exist for learning sportsmanship, conduct and fair play, it is coaches who establish, teach and model the standard of expectations.

For those twelve through eighteen years of age, the rewards of participating in sports at the physical education and recreational levels are still intrinsic — for personal satisfaction. The expectation of future high-value extrinsic rewards (money, scholarships) is not a key factor for most. However, even within the refreshing amateurism of youth sports, the desire to excel just for the sake of the contest, is beginning to be eroded by the overuse of external rewards and glorification of winning.

7

The Parents' Role as Teacher in Youth Sports

The influence of parents or guardians on their children's success in sports can't be overemphasized. From start to finish they have the option of making it either a quality-filled lifelong experience or one remembered for its stress.

By following a few simple rules recognizing the necessity to keep fun in the picture while overseeing youth in their sports, you can help organize athletic activities in a fashion young people will appreciate. It doesn't matter whether or not participation is of a recreational nature or in more competitive sports — the player is the prize. Keeping sight of that prize puts winning into proper perspective. There's nothing wrong with winning, but for most youngsters, "fun" is the object.

Winning for the scoreboard should not be the major goal. If positive values are not taught to youngsters, then all their wins count for little. Few of your children's future jobs, friends or relationships will be based on their win-loss record while they were in grade school, high school or college. It won't make any difference! What's really important is the type of people they become. The parents' role is to steer their children into teams or programs which have healthy environments.

Remember, you are the parents of the athlete for only a short time, but you are parents forever. Blocking ability in football, shooting percentages in basketball, or running speed in track are not enduring traits; the values young athletes learn are.

The Parent as an Advocate

Following is one example of how parents can become effective advocates for their children:

An eighth-grade boy who wasn't playing often enough on his baseball team was getting ready to quit. He knew he was not the best, and his low opinion of himself affected his performance as shortstop. Still, he came to practice, demonstrated a great attitude and thought that counted for something. Finally, he and his parents discussed his feelings and decided the best solution was for the boy to approach the coach and ask: "What do I need to do to get better so that I can play more?"

The coach, not expecting the question and caught at a harried moment, gave the boy a lame response and dismissed him. The boy left in tears, determined to leave the team.

The parents did not want the boy to be denied the basic right of at least getting a fair answer to a legitimate question and prepared themselves for a second approach to the coach. They wanted to review their son's practice habits, role on the team, capability and goals, while also honoring their son's caveat not to make a scene.

The parents and the surprised coach arrived at an equitable solution, which did not translate directly into more playing time for the boy, but it provided a time for improvement for the boy which called for extra effort from him, the parents and the coach. By season's end, the boy got to play more, the parents were proud of their son's improvement, and the coach became better at his job.

If these parents had not acted as advocates, if they had sat back and not asserted themselves, their son may have developed a significant sense of inferiority which may have had a long-term negative impact. Being an effective advocate of youth sports requires understanding the situation, diplomacy, judgment, skill and playing by the rules. Here are some suggestions for becoming a good advocate:

Knowing Everyone's Roles
With all the pressure parents face today as supervisors, role models, inspirational teachers, and as loving adults for their children, how can they be expected to know how to guide their children's sports activities? How can they be the best advocates?

The answers to these questions are one of the fundamental reasons for this book. It's offered as a guide to parents to help them make the right decisions. The authors, both parents with coaching and sports teaching backgrounds, know the dilemma of parents and have made it less burdensome by providing valuable information in a structured form.

Parents should not be expected to know all the ins and outs of athletic philosophy, sports law, due process, eligi-

bility, discipline, safety standards, injury care, team conduct
code, coaches' qualifications, insurance, and so on. In order
to understand how to help, parents first need to be aware of
their role in the player-coach partnership, and also the roles
the other partners play. These are bewildering subjects for
parents. How these, and other concerns, have been identified by the Tahoma School District (see page 157) is a fine
reference for parents who need an introduction to the idea
of sports as well as definite answers.

Save the Day

Prioritize the Day

Make a five-minute habit each morning, or before
going to bed, to list the coming day's agenda. Prioritize
the list of tasks. The 1's indicate must accomplish
before the day's end; 2's mean you must take action; 3's
are tasks you hope to get started. Circle the "1" that is
easiest to accomplish and start your day with it. As your
day progresses, cross off items when completed.

Repeat the process for the next day by first
advancing the unfinished items to your next day's list of
tasks. If you have advanced an item three times, toss it
or delegate it.

Post your day for Team Family to see.

Being an Effective Teacher

Considered by many to be a coaches' model, John
Wooden, former UCLA basketball coach, had a philosophy
based on doing small things correctly. His books and videos
point out that if a player learned to execute the basics, he
would be successful. Primary among the beliefs Wooden
stood by was that outstanding teachers/coaches have

common characteristics. An advocate can learn from coaches who use John Wooden's techniques:

1. *Give choices.* Allow athletes a voice in setting limits on intensity and length of time spent on sports.
2. *Be brief.* Most players have short attention spans. Be aware of facial expressions; you'll know when they've had enough.
3. *Don't lecture.* Players want to know why as well as what needs to be learned. Action rather than words will mean more to most youngsters.
4. *Clarify.* Continually ask, "What do you think I am trying to say?" A good idea is to ask players to repeat what they thought you said. Don't be judgmental.
5. *Demonstrate.* If you can perform the skill, show it. If you can't, don't. Those unable to demonstrate basic skills have many options, including sports-related videos from the library and they have the option of asking a neighbor, friend or relative to lend a hand.
6. *Don't expect too much too soon.*
7. *Use all tools.* (Visual, verbal, hands-on, repetition, trial and error, etc.)
8. *Praise.* A generous helping will accomplish wonders with players and will keep it fun.
9. *Provide feedback.* Let children show you what they've learned in the past and how good they've become at that skill. Ask them what they did right every day.

Of course, this advice is not only good for coaches, but it applies equally well to parents who have the ability to coach their players at home and are interested in helping their children get the most from sports.

Good   teachers recognize the need to allow for mistakes, which can become a major stepping stone to later successes.

Good teachers also recognize the need to meet the expectations of those being taught. We've seen the importance of fun to young players, so it's essential that organized or at-home practices teach how to have fun, they also need to be fun!

Community coaches and parents without specific teaching experience need to read books on how to teach before reading books on how to coach. A prominent coach tells his workshop audiences: "If you have time to read only one book on coaching, find a good one on how to teach!"

It's important to differentiate between "fun" and "wasting time." It's not fun to let the players run the practices and do what they want all the time — they need at least some direction, even if it isn't obvious; otherwise, practice will get out of hand and become a waste of time. Even the most non-competitive teams/leagues need to provide adult instruction on skills, tactics, etc.

Good Parenting Capitalizes on Mistakes

Intimidation or sarcasm isn't effective with a child and will encourage resentment and withdrawal. Knowing what to teach and when to teach is important. It's obvious an eight-year-old can't perform as well as someone two or three years older, so don't set goals so high that they are not achievable. Also, work on only a few things at a time. Otherwise young people (old ones also) can spread themselves too thin, and progress is slowed rather than escalated. Remember to reward achievement.

Coaching youngsters in sessions apart from formal practice is an opportunity which, if handled properly, increases the bond between parent and child, and it permits the child to test his skills and apply them later under actual game conditions. Gaining confidence leads to risk-taking. From risks come mistakes, and from mistakes comes proficiency. If any of these elements are removed from the process, the young person is not getting a chance to succeed. Don't be critical of mistakes. Without them there is no progress.

Good Parenting Gives Positive Reinforcement

How something is said is equally important as what is said. There are numerous ways to transmit information; one of the more common mistakes by parents/coaches is using one or more of the following phrases in the name of "motivation" when, in reality, they may be putting unnecessary negative influences on young athletes.

In most cases, using positive comments and pointing out specific accomplishments will do more than a constant pushing for perfection. Choose an appropriate phrase and follow it up with specific ideas on "how" and "why" they will be beneficial. Present this information in a way the player will understand what's expected and what specific rewards will be generated from better practices/games.

Sample phrases (from parents or coaches) that stop the learning process:

1. What's wrong with you? Haven't we done this a million times before?
2. How many times do I have to tell you...?
3. If you'd only think about it, you'd know what to do.
4. If that's the best you can do, maybe you should just quit the team.
5. It's obvious you never bother to practice.
6. You're bigger and stronger than your friends, yet they are playing more and you are warming the bench.

7. When I was your age, I knew all the basics and my parents never spent all the time and money we're spending on you.

8. Even though you had a good game, if you had done your best you would feel much better about yourself.

9. Your (brother/sister/neighbor) would have stopped her player from scoring the winning goal.

10. I'll give you two dollars for every goal you score. If you don't score any, you can't go to the neighbor's party.

Try these instead:

1. You put out a great effort. No one can ask for much more than that!

2. I really appreciate all the extra time and effort you put into learning this game.

3. I really enjoy having you on this team.

4. If I can help you, let me know. If I can't, I'll find someone who can.

5. Don't worry about making mistakes; that's how you learn.

6. You can do it!

7. Great effort! You have improved tremendously since you first started working on that skill.

8. You are a quick learner; that's something a lot of people would like to be.

9. Thank you for giving the team your best effort.

10. Just because you missed a shot is no reason to stop shooting.

Don't promise something you can't deliver! Whether as coach or parent, don't tell young athletes that if they do something, they will definitely get more playing time if you are not absolutely certain it will happen. If unsure, don't promise — you won't be believed in the future, and the best of intentions will turn sour.

Know When to Get Out of the Way

Other than cases of physical abuse or gross misbehavior on the part of the coach, which call for immediate action, parents should always consider the right place and time to talk to the coach. Diplomacy and courtesy are good rules to follow. There are a number of situations after both winning and losing games when inappropriate behavior by parents can cause permanent emotional damage for themselves and their player. Picking the right time and place to talk to the coach, as well as the right message to deliver, is important. We are not aware of any situation in which a youngster benefited from uncalled-for behavior by his parents. At a minimum, the parents are thoroughly embarrassed; at worst, they can only save face by forcing the child to quit the team.

The Tahoma School District Study

The Tahoma School District Athletic/Activities Task Force, founded in 1995, believes the values and attitudes learned and taught to student participants of interscholastic activities has been proven to be important to success in life. Based on this research, the task force identified specific program outcomes/attitudes and expectations students should be taught.

"Stakeholders" were named by the task force. These were people who had a significant contribution to make to the achievement of the desired outcomes. They were identified as coaches, student participants, parents, teachers, the community, and administrators.

The primary purpose of the co-curricular activity program of the Tahoma School District, the task force stated, was to promote the physical, mental, aesthetic, social, emotional and moral well-being of students through sports participation and competition. From their participation, the task force believed, youngsters would gain experiences that would improve their:

1. Self-actualization and self-esteem.
2. Positive attitudes and ability to have fun.
3. Work ethic, goal setting, skills and commitment.
4. Skills development and citizenship values (personal character traits).
5. Development of a win-win attitude.
6. Opportunities to benefit from a variety of leadership styles and participation.
7. Competitive spirit.
8. Leadership.

A partnership of all stakeholders was emphasized by the task force, and the partnership nature was clarified by a chart that outlined roles and expectations for each of the participants.

Since parents and coaches are primary to the learning experience of students, the chart defined activities and responsibilities each group would assume.

To Teach:	Coaches Should:	Parents Should:
1. Self-Esteem	Reinforce athletes' successes Emphasize goal attainment Recognize all contributions Discipline so as to not degrade Dress appropriately for game and practice	Be good listeners Make a support commitment Recognize the best effort of your children Establish progressive goals
2. Positive Attitude	Promote team-building activities Display positive attitude	Organize and join support groups Attend contest, functions, events Live your talk; be positive yourself
3. Fun	Provide participation for all	Be involved yourself for fun
4. Work Ethic (Responsibility and Commitment)	Answer all parent questions, especially those dealing with depth of commitment. Model work ethic, leadership, punctuality and persistence in team goals.	Cooperate with players and coach to encourage work ethic. They should understand the time commitment and support team rules, and support team goal Show trust, and expect trust
5. Skill Development	Know skills Break down skills into participant's level Provide a variety of skill development tools: tapes, videos, books.	Ask coach what skills are needed and become familiar with those skills Work with your athletes at home.
6. Win-Win Relationships	Help participants realize their full potential Teach the basics while building a cooperative team environment Teach a desire for students to perform their best without the fear of losing Show respect for opponents and sense of fair play	Establish a "sense of value" and support program in positive ways Build good relations and a loving atmosphere Insist on knowing the rules and playing by them

An Advocate's Do's and Don'ts

In addition, the task force developed a list of Do's and Don'ts for adults in organized youth activities.

Do	*Don't*
Do become available to youth.	Don't model disinterest.
Do communicate problems to leadership.	Don't verbally attack confidences your child imparts to you.
Do walk your talk with constructive ideas.	Don't criticize things you don't know about.
Do start a home support team.	Don't ignore family values.
Do attend your child's activity.	Don't criticize the quality of skill/talent your child exhibits.
Do seek answers to concerns/questions you have.	Don't assume you know the reasons for everything.
Do enjoy the time you spend with your child in his sport.	Don't give false, reluctant time.
Do thank the positive role models.	Don't embarrass yourself by improper behavior.
Do prioritize important goals for youth.	Don't place win/lose above all else.
Do keep a long-term perspective.	Don't end the journey because of one flat tire.

Emphasized by the task force was the message: We adults control the learning experiences of youth activities. The criteria to measure the success of youth-organized activities are the outcomes/attitudes/values gained by those for whom the program operates, not the operators of the program. Learning is a lifelong activity. The losers resulting from adult failures in teamwork are those being led — the students.

It should be apparent from the goals, guidelines and ideas developed by the Tahoma Washington Task Force that primary among the constituents responsible for developing the character, values and playing spirit of youths in sport are parents and coaches.

Responses from a 1995 survey of thousands of players, parents and coaches of high school teams conducted by one of the authors demonstrated the expectations these separate groups had for the players as members of a team.

What Parents Want for Players
Players Should:
- Feel good about themselves
- Be treated fairly
- Be given a chance to prove their ability
- Learn new skills

What Players Want from Coaches
Players Want to:
- Receive good instruction
- Feel good about themselves (self-worth)
- Share in decision-making
- Learn new skills

What Coaches Expect
Coaches Expect to:
- Teach life skills (including teamwork)
- Earn respect and support from players, parents and community
- Develop character in players
- Teach players how to win and how to lose

We believe that if the members of each group shown above accept a partnership role, the chance of misunderstandings that can lead to negative sports press will be minimized, and emphasis on the value of sports will come to the forefront.

It is almost axiomatic, we have discovered, that if there is imbalance in the three-way partnership of player, parents and coach, then the partner who feels most threatened will dictate the mood of the team and everyone associated with it.

Many coaches attribute a team's success to the positive support it gets from its parental support base. Humiliating other people's children or yelling at officials does not qualify as positive cheering. Parents create a positive atmosphere by restricting their cheering to expressions of support for team and player. That's what players want to hear. It does little good for them to hear any negative cheering.

Parents do have a right to make recommendations as to the physical expectations coaches make on youngsters, particularly those at earlier ages. More than most volunteer coaches, parents are aware of the endurance and performance their child can tolerate. They must communicate this information to coaches. Without this input, coaches often assume there are no limitations and will aspire to greater skill development for a child than should be reasonably expected. If there is a learning disability of any nature, the coach must be notified.

Parents who are centered on their child's winning above all else must be prepared for both elation and disappointment. If their child happens to be one of the few who beats the odds and gets the scholarship or professional contract, that's rewarding. However, less than three percent of all athletes who compete ever do. Parents need to be realistic in preparing themselves and their daughter/son for disappointment. Most young people, by the time they are in high school, have figured out for themselves what their chances are, but if they are pushed unrealistically by parents, they may often see themselves as failures. A failure at eighteen?

Parenting and the Team Family Concept

The next progression beyond the "partnership" is to recognize the strength that family adds to the successful sports program.

Team Family is a concept that provides a cooperative matrix within which members of the family can interact to help players in the family become more effective at their sports. Properly put into action, this concept can induce in the family circle a higher sense of group loyalty, increased pride for each member, strength, and ties of love and devotion. Sports as a centerpiece for family discussion cannot be underestimated.

Bill and Betty Volpentest are proud parents of six children. Tony, the youngest, born without feet or hands, joined his brothers and sisters as an equal member of an active and sharing family. As in any family, Tony learned the importance of determination and attitude when defining personal success.

As a high school sophomore, Tony decided, although advised to seek realistic non-sport challenges, to join the high school track team as a sprinter! From a humble beginning of last-place finishes in junior varsity sprint events, Tony persisted and lettered in track his senior year.

Tony Volpentest graduated from high school in 1991 with the respect and admiration of all who watched him run and those who heard him encourage all athletes to "do it drug free" and "by the rules."

During the 1992 Para-Olympics in Barcelona, Spain, Tony Volpentest was a double gold medalist, setting two world records: the 100 meters in 11.63 seconds, and the 200 meters in 23.07 seconds. He lowered both world records several times en route to repeating as a double gold medalist in 1996 at the Atlanta Para-Olympics. Tony runs with the aid of prostheses, determination, and self-respect — the latter two being most important.

How Do Parents Teach and Motivate Their Athletes?

An alternative to criticism is to look for something positive to praise. Even after a very poor performance, a Team Family motivates by recognizing:

Players Don't Need Threats of Punishment to Motivate Them

- Athletes want to do well; motivation is part of the intrinsic challenge.

- Poor performance and bad luck are best accepted when the disappointment is shared.
- Punishment or criticism rarely motivates anyone other than the punisher, and certainly won't motivate children.
- The player who performed poorly does not need to be reminded — nobody knows it better than he does.

Withholding a Reward Motivates Only Those Who Want the Reward

- Enjoyment and intrinsic awards, according to teenagers, are the most effective.
- The main objective of disciplinary action should be to correct and remediate undesirable behavior.

Keeping Rewards and Consequences Balanced

Team Family should understand that everybody enjoys recognition of some sort. Coaches and parents achieve positive results when they reward trying, not just achievement. Too often only outcome is recognized as a reason to celebrate. Dispersing large doses of praise when intermediate performance steps towards goals are met encourages additional effort. While working with your player, set up a system of rewards when certain physical or mental goals have been met. A progress chart hung on the wall, a computer-generated program designed for your child, an unexpected gift, a surprise trip to a movie, or an extra treat at dinner — all serve the purpose of rewarding effort.

Many people, after quitting a job or retiring, remember the lack of praise on the job as the most outstanding fault with their former employer. People thrive on compliments, on recognition of their achievements, big or small. All too often praise of a player is withheld until an outcome is achieved, when praise along the way would be more productive. Waiting for outcome as the only criteria for reward limits achievement. Youngsters need constant praise, whether they are in sports, at school, or at home. Praise builds confidence and heightens the desire for accomplishment.

Also, it is important to give specific praise as reward. Saying, "Nice job," after practice loses its effectiveness when constantly repeated because it is too general, but congratulations for improvement in a specific, named, skill pays big dividends. "Great blocking! Your practice work is paying off," is a more effective way of making a player feel appreciated.

Building Player Self-Esteem

The parents in Team Family are also cheerleaders and ego builders. Coaches at the collegiate level report that low self-esteem, when it is present, can usually be traced back to excessive negative input during childhood from adults who rarely expressed satisfaction with the youth's performance. Many players feel insecure and show a history of failure because they think they've never met people's expectations. Often these feelings can point to misguided early adult help and are rarely born of a parent's desire to be negative. Seldom does a player need to be reminded that he has played a bad game. Players know better than anybody who missed the last shot, misjudged the finish line, stayed up too late the night before competing, fumbled at a critical time, or lost concentration. The player always knows!

Helpful advice should be deferred until the player can absorb the positive intent of a performance critique. Good cheerleaders know when to cheer and when to keep quiet.

How many adults perform in front of their peers or family? While you may work for someone who puts much emphasis on reviewing quality and timeliness of your efforts, rarely are adults under constant observation. Rarer still is a workplace where errors of judgment are loudly booed and success is cheered. These are reserved for sports and other extracurricular activities. The most demanding and least competitive sports programs have one thing in common: the youngsters, the ones with the least maturity, are performing and risking in front of those with the most maturity. The ability to handle the acclaim and disapproval in a positive way will produce healthy egos.

Constant criticism or over-adulation produces poor self-image. Reward the youngster by showing you appreciated his performance. He wants to know that there was some observable value in what he did. After all, what player sets out to sabotage his team by making mistakes on purpose? He will appreciate a "good effort" far more than a "you should have...."

There is always time later to work on developing skills which will help avoid mistakes in the future. A compliment now lasts a long time.

A final reminder: It is important to recognize the difference between correctable and uncontrollable mistakes, which can be confused with negativism and coaching. Coaching at school or in Team Family involves direction and repetition. Without direction and repetition, bad habits develop. While some players may perceive direction and repetition as negatives, they are intended as the opposite. Perception is everything. If a child or teenager thinks coaching by a parent or another person is negative, then in his mind it is. A major step is assisting your child in a positive and non-threatening way. If he thinks practice with his parents is fun and is truly helpful, then in his mind it will be. It is the way an event is perceived, not the event itself, which creates the attitude.

Team Family Failures: Poor Parental Behavior at Games

It seems to be a national trend that fans at any kind of sports event have become more negative, not only to officials, but also to other players on their child's team. Listening to hurled comments, criticism and badmouthing gives newer players' parents the impression that the way to cheer is to berate everyone in sight. Some feel comfortable in the "big-mouth" role and add to the problem. But parents need to realize that fan behavior is their contribution to team unity. The following anecdote illustrates what can happen when passion for a sport gets out of hand:

A forty-five-year-old Little League coach was convicted of assault with a deadly weapon (an aluminum baseball bat) for hitting an umpire twice during a May 16 post-game argument. The umpire had called the game because of darkness, which reverted (by rule) the score to the last full inning, when the other team was winning. The umpire's head wounds were closed with forty stitches. The jury deliberated more than three hours to obtain a conviction.

All the written contracts and words about self-image, fun, positive attitude, accountability and success mean nothing to young people who observe adults misbehaving and being rude at games. Once children connect the lack of proper behavior and courtesy in adults to team goals, then value statements meant to guide children become words without substance. Mature participation at youth sporting events is the sole responsibility of all parents. Players and coaches ultimately bear the brunt of improper behavior (games have been forfeited due to moms and dads who got out of control). And a number of coaches have quit because they have felt rude parents have been uncontrollable. The fact is, acting foolish, boorish, overbearing, loud, insulting and interjective is a sign of gross immaturity, and if players respond on the playing floor in the same inappropriate fashion, no one can be blamed but the rude rolemakers whose performances have been copied.

If a parent/guardian becomes aware of inappropriate behavior by another parent, he must take immediate corrective action. Left unchecked, rudeness will have a direct influence on your own son/daughter no matter how good a fan you may be. Sound judgment and the knowledge that other parents feel the same way about boorish behavior will give responsible adults the courage to take appropriate action in a timely manner. It is a shared responsibility of all the parents, coaches, officials and administrators to correct abnormal fans, not just the coaches! Parents can't wait for someone else to solve the problem and often need to take the initiative. A phone call or joint meeting with other concerned parents will be a solid, positive first step and often the only step required.

As with any interpersonal relationship, if you must contact parent offenders to ask them to refrain from improper behavior and remarks, setting the stage is important before meeting with them. We've discovered that in almost all cases the fans are unaware of their influence and will react in a positive way to constructive criticism. Parents who have been corrected diplomatically often will start directing their comments in a truly positive way and add to the success of the program. Be stingy with finding fault at almost every turn, or else players and fans will simply withdraw. Look for the positive. Don't become a fault finder ... they always find what they're looking for! Outcome-based fans often are not outcome-based in their workplace or at home. Getting them to modify their behavior is not as difficult as you may imagine.

Following is an example of a parent who went too far, which serves to illustrate the observations we have made:

The girls' basketball contest came to a dramatic end when the opponents made a last-second shot, and the comeback fell one point short. Players on both teams shook hands, and coaches exchanged sincere congratulations for a well-played game. While the game was for the league championship, it was well played, and everybody realized that the winning basket was actually quite a feat of luck. Disappointed, but with dignity, the losing team left the floor. It was a tough loss, and they felt "the agony of defeat." Across the court, however, a parent had to be restrained from provoking a fight with one of the referees, and later he was dragged out of the gym, cursing and shouting. Observing this incident, the losing players became agitated and started blaming everyone from the coach to their best friends for their loss. Suddenly it had become impossible for them to separate losing from failure when, just a few minutes earlier, they had felt the satisfaction of having done their best, a feeling which had taken the sting out of losing.

We often wondered if the referee worked another game involving the losing team and what action, if any, the parents of the team members took to eliminate disruptions at future games. This team of sixth-grade girls experienced fan behavior at its worst.

In another case, following a disappointing loss, a basketball coach was approached by a parent of the opposing team and was told, "If I were you and got all those terrible calls from the refs, I would have started throwing chairs. If you had, I'm sure our fans would have been totally out of control. I really admire your restraint. You and the kids acted with a lot of class."

Many things can be learned from losing. In this case, the reactions of players and coach were recognized as examples of restraint and courtesy in the face of questionable referee calls. Perhaps everyone in the gym that day learned a valuable lesson.

Team Family Management Tips

Team Family time management is important today because of the demands on moms and dads. Following is a salute to Team Family moms, after which are Team Family management tips that parents will find useful.

WANTED: FOOTBALL MOMS

Applicants must be willing to spend twenty-four hours a day living football; give up weekends; give sons to coaches from August to December. Applicants must give instant repair to: uniforms, skinned knees, sprained egos, broken promises, bad calls, and broken dates, be cheerleaders Friday nights, accept referees, suffer weathermen, and believe sportswriters even when they are illogical.

High school Football Moms must smile when they would rather cry, pump up footballs and pride, keep meals warm for hours, serve mobs of starving teenagers without notice, provide midnight taxi service and complete food passes as people dash out doorways, show enthusiasm during freezing weather while sitting on metal bleachers, smile while soaking wet.

Football Moms must accept sons that go 90 m.p.h. on Fridays and 2 m.p.h. mowing lawns on Saturday, must be willing to learn a foreign language and know a bingo from a bcat, a dive from a trap, belly from flat, stingers, focus, snap, rover, blood left, red dog, crack-backs, blind sides.

Moms need to meet all emergencies yesterday, wash uniforms, cars, socks and other necessities, have tireless energy, love whole teams, suffer silently in defeat, leave applause to others after victory, never yell "Defense" when her son's team has the ball, always agree with dads and referees and other dumb-dumbs, never complain, and only mentally hit people with an umbrella.

If applicants for Football Moms will step forward, with winning smile, unlimited enthusiasm, faultless dedication, sacrifice all personal desires, watch small boys grow to men on a practice field, suffer silently with every injury or defeat, leave the joys of victory to others, and say, "I WOULD LOVE A JOB LIKE THAT," they will be considered for a 1996 position with Football Moms.

Parents'/Guardians' Code of Conduct

All parents should follow a code of conduct that merges the responsibilities of managing Team Family with the obligations of being involved in youth sports. Here is an example code:

As an overseer of a child participating in youth sports, I will attempt to provide the following support:

• Communicate with coaches in appropriate settings to discuss matters of concern.

• Transport players to and from activities on a timely basis.

• Support the coaches' code regarding use of drugs, alcohol and tobacco. (The age at which youth start using drugs has consistently fallen so cooperation with the coach is essential.)

• Volunteer to assist in whatever way possible to make our players' sporting activities a positive experience, for them and for Team Family members.

• Recognize that no one is perfect, and as long as everyone associated with the team works positively toward meeting team objectives, the team will learn values of teamwork and have fun and success.

• Actively participate in promoting good sportsmanship toward all players, other parents, officials and opponents at team events.

• Rely upon praise instead of negative criticism to produce behavior changes.

Sports Information Bank Checklist
Information parents should have and how to get it

1. Attend pre-season meeting and obtain copies of:
   ___ Organization philosophy and policies
   ___ Program goals and purposes
   ___ Eligibility standards and regulations
   ___ Codes and player requirements of:
       ___ Team   ___ Organization/School
       ___ State/National
   ___ Discipline policies and process
       ___ Procedures   ___ Appeals   ___ Actions
   ___ Communications network and methods
       ___ Parents' contact   ___ Coaches' contact
       ___ Protocol and procedures to and
       from family

2. Ask coaches for practice requirements, plans, schedules:
   ___ Dates, location, and times of practices/games
   ___ Academic accommodations for players
       ___ Team goals   ___ Incentives
       ___ Expectations
       ___ Excused absence from practices policy
   ___ Team travel policies
   ___ Game day procedures and situations
       ___ Player requirements; expectations of parents
       ___ Travel codes   ___ Requirements
       ___ Absences

3. From athletic director receive help and information for:

___ Medical treatment of players' policy
___ Insurance coverage
___ Camps and out-of-season expectations
___ Players' conduct policies away from sport
___ Media coverage and official notices
___ Coaches' criteria for rating players

4. Obtain copies of goals and expectations from coaches:
   ___ Program philosophy and mission
   ___ Team   ___ Coaches   ___ Season
   ___ Support groups   ___ Post-season activities
   ___ Awards and qualifying criteria
   ___ Decision-making process and procedures

5. Prepare written questions regarding special concerns:
   ___ Discussed with family prior to presenting?
   ___ Copy presented to _____ Date _____

6. ___ Keep home Sports Information Bank file available

Post-season Parent Evaluation Form

The final parent responsibility is to evaluate the season and provide this information to those who need it. Through constant evaluation and fine tuning as is appropriate, all of the stakeholders in youth sports can create the best possible programs. The following form will be helpful for parents, both for their own family's benefit and to share with appropriate organizations/officials.

‒ ▪ ‒ ▪ ‒ ▪ ‒ ▪ ‒ ▪ ‒ ▪ ‒ ▪ ‒ ▪ ‒ ▪ ‒ ▪ ‒ ▪ ‒ ▪ ‒ ▪

Post-season Parent Evaluation Form

A. Evaluate the degree to which you believe your son or daughter achieved the following:
(circle one – Very Much, Somewhat, Not at All):

My child had fun	VM	S	NA
My child learned the fundamentals of the sport	VM	S	NA
Our family had fun	VM	S	NA

B. Evaluate the degree to which you believe your child changed on the following characteristics:
(circle one – Improved, No Change, Declined, Don't Know):

Physical fitness	I	NC	D	DK
Learning to cooperate	I	NC	D	DK
Self-confidence	I	NC	D	DK
Desire to continue playing this sport	I	NC	D	DK
Self-esteem	I	NC	D	DK
Learning specific skills of this sport	I	NC	D	DK
Leadership skills	I	NC	D	DK
Sportsmanship	I	NC	D	DK
Learning to take initiative	I	NC	D	DK
Learning to compete	I	NC	D	DK

C. Evaluate how the coach did on the following items:
(circle one – Excellent, Good, So-So, Weak, Poor, Don't Know):

Treated your child fairly	E	G	SS	W	P	DK
Kept winning in perspective	E	G	SS	W	P	DK
Took safety precautions	E	G	SS	W	P	DK

Organized practice/contests	E	G	SS	W	P	DK
Communicated with you	E	G	SS	W	P	DK
Effective in teaching skills	E	G	SS	W	P	DK
Encouraged your child	E	G	SS	W	P	DK
Recognized your child as a unique individual	E	G	SS	W	P	DK
Held your child's respect	E	G	SS	W	P	DK

D. How did we do as parents on the following:
(circle one – Excellent, Good, So-So, Weak, Poor, Don't Know):

Offered help to coaches	E	G	SS	W	P	DK
Listened to our child's sports talk	E	G	SS	W	P	DK

Provided logistical support
    (transportation,
    equipment fees)
	E	G	SS	W	P	DK

Showed enthusiasm	E	G	SS	W	P	DK
Assisted away from practice	E	G	SS	W	P	DK
Helped our child learn new skills	E	G	SS	W	P	DK

E. Please give any additional comments in the space below and on the back. (Perhaps you have some constructive criticism or praise you want to offer.)

8

The Road to Victory

Families who have already experienced an introduction to sports, we hope in the manner suggested in Chapter Two, should be looking forward to an extended journey as their young athletes progress along the many sports avenues available to them. The family will discover many roadside attractions — unexpected events to enjoy — along the sports road, as well as potholes, most of which can be avoided through family planning.

Parents, as leaders of Team Family, are responsible that the (sports) trip is enjoyed by all family members and they arrive safely at the planned destination. To achieve this purpose, we recommend the following five steps:

1. Clarify Expectations: What does everyone want to accomplish on the trip?
2. Maintain Positive Attitudes: Keep all traveling partners in a good mood.
3. Measure Progress: Are we traveling fast enough? Too fast? In the right direction?

4. Evaluate Results: Are we getting what we expected?
5. Choose an alternate route when the main road is blocked.

Clarify Expectation

Before family members get involved in a specific sports activity, it is wise for the family to reach an understanding of what each member will be committing to. The family can work through this process in many ways; however, we recommend an approach many families have found to be insightful, productive and fun.

This tried-and-true approach involves writing a "sports commercial" which will turn out to be a prediction of how the season will unfold. More than just a prediction, the commercial is a directional blueprint which shows who must do what to make the forecast come true, thereby strengthening the family's goals.

To understand the real benefit of writing a commercial, please examine the two samples that follow. One is written by a fourteen-year-old boy who wishes to develop as a soccer player. The next is written by the boy's parents, who declare their intention to help their son achieve his goal.

Player's Sports Commercial

I am Paul, a 14-year-old who enjoys playing soccer. I would like someday to be a high school varsity goalkeeper and, in order to do so, I know there are certain things I need to do.

• Stay in good physical and mental condition and maintain a healthy lifestyle.

- Maintain my grade-point average while I'm spending more time at sports.
- Keep sports in perspective; I will not knowingly violate my family's values and will make every effort to attend important family functions.
- Play by the rules of team and coach as long as they don't conflict with my personal beliefs or my family's.

Playing high school soccer has been a goal of mine ever since my first game seven years ago. I know many who have played for our school, and I want to experience the fun and excitement they tell me about. My school has not been too good at soccer, and I'd like a chance to help them improve their standings in the league.

I also want to play baseball and run track, because I am good at those too. Because of this, I don't think I want to go to summer camps or play soccer all year long, or else I'd never get good at other sports.

It's important for me to play sports, because I can learn a lot about myself and how to become a leader. In order to do this, I am willing to play hard, learn by watching older players, work with my coach and my neighbor (who used to be a goalkeeper), and watch films/videos on how to be a good player.

I would like my parents to help me with my soccer and hope they can come and cheer for me and my team. I would be embarrassed if they were like some other parents who constantly yell at officials and the other teams. I would like them to be positive and help me be positive too. Their support, whether we win or lose, is important to me.

Parents' Sports Commercial

As Paul's parents, we want to help him reach his goals, while also giving him guidance and direction by teaching him that there is a lot more to sports than winning games. We would like him to have fun, learn about self-sufficiency, and the value of teamwork.

We respect the personal goals he has set for himself and will help him reach these even if he decides not to play high school soccer.

It is important to us that one sport does not dominate Paul's life. We want him to participate in many sports at this time of his life so that if and when the time comes to pick a favorite, he will be able to make a good decision.

We have given Paul exposure to other extracurricular activities and will continue to do so, because we think he has real talent in track and baseball. But he also is an excellent leader, and we'd like to see him develop this characteristic in other school organizations.

If Paul needs to attend camps, play on select teams, play all year long, or give up all other sports, then we would need to discuss his ambitions to play high school soccer further. We will work with him to find out exactly what's expected by the school coach and help him make the right choice before he starts getting overly committed.

We will support Paul in a positive way and be there for him.

You will note that in the two commercials shown here, player and parents are in basic agreement. Quite often, however, parents and children do not agree. Thus, commercials can focus on differences and allow parents and player to make necessary adjustments to their expectations.

Now that you have read these commercials, turn next to the six questions, one set each for player and parents. When you supply the answers to these questions, you will have provided yourself with material upon which to base your commercial. This applies just as well to the parents as it does to their player.

Whether or not you write a formal "commercial," the exercise of putting your thoughts on paper will clarify your objectives in sports participation.

Questions for the Player

1. Why do you think it's important to be in sports?
2. At what level do you think you wish to compete? Why?
3. How much support do you expect from parents/ guardian?
4. Are you willing to commit to "practice away from practice" if your coach encourages it?
5. How do you define success?
6. Will you be a success in life if you don't achieve your sports goals?

Questions for the Parents

1. How do you view sports? (What emphasis do you put on them, and why?)
2. How will they meet family expectations?
3. What benefit do you expect your player to gain from sports competition?

4. Can he or she get the same benefit from other activities?

5. How will you assist your youngster in reaching his goals?

6. How do you define success?

What's the practical value of the sports commercial you have written? The answer is that if you compare your commercial with the sports programs available to you, you can more easily determine if there is a good match between your expectations and the reality of the specific activity. The intent of this whole, simple process is to synchronize the expectations of parents, players, and the sports program under consideration. The commercial you've written is groundwork for building a good partnership.

Save the Day

Guarantee: Enjoy Thirty Minutes of Each Day

Set aside time during the day to do an enjoyable task. If possible, plan to break up unpleasant tasks with ones you enjoy. Schedule an enjoyable activity during work breaks. Phone an old friend, trace a picture, create a silly gizmo, rename your children. You will be amazed at your own creativity.

Record and periodically review the activities with high enjoyment values.

Building and Maintaining Positive Attitudes

Good coaches know if they create an environment in which players maintain a positive attitude, the team will be successful, not only in the win/lose column, but also in the victories of life. An essential ingredient in all inspirational success stories (the rags-to-riches, miraculous-healing, contribution-to-mankind, and the love-overcomes-all stories) is a dominant positive attitude. A positive attitude is an emotional manner of behaving that combines a healthy portion of positive expectation, desire, self-confidence, and a dash of joy.

Witnessing a positive attitude in children is the number one indicator that they are benefiting from sports (or any other activity). A good attitude generally confirms that a young player is experiencing fun, learning new skills, and enjoying teammates. The ultimate result of sports is to build healthier individuals, families and communities. To accomplish this, the emphasis must be on developing an attitude of "I can do it." "This is fun." "My parents and coach are really trying to help me." or, "I'm getting better every day."

Parents who take an active and positive interest in their children's sports activities are confirming the value of those activities. This is the kick-off point of modeling positive attitude. Like sponges, children soak up the attitudes of those around them. Parents who enthusiastically help with practice at home — if that is a part of the family's sports involvement — are modeling positive attitude. Associating with positive people is the most important principle in maintaining positive attitudes ourselves.

Occasionally two parents will not agree on the level of play for their child; one will want a competitive program, the other a non-competitive recreational program. Reconciling their differences and presenting a unified voice will help the child maintain a positive attitude. Young people are tuned-in; they can spot the different expectations from Mom and Dad but are caught in the middle. One escape route is to drop sports and get out of the tension-filled middle ground. If parents have a unified voice which is completely different from the coaches, the child is again caught in the middle. By now you know our central conviction: the family comes first. Family first is a policy parents need to impress upon the coach so that the child doesn't feel torn between two conflicting loyalties.

To help young athletes maintain a positive attitude, coaches and parents need to show their support during times when the youngster is playing well, and also when he is not. Consistent parental support bolsters a player's self-esteem with the result that youth, fortified with encouragement from parents and others, feel more positive about everything. There is a popular saying, "Whether you think you can, or think you can't...you are right." To paraphrase Yogi Berra, that part of sports which is half mental makes 90 percent of the difference.

The selection of program and coach has a crucial effect on a young player's sports attitude. If a player constantly complains about the majority of things at practice or games, it's time to take a second look at the whole picture and consider attitude adjustments. Positive attitude generally has been accepted as being the best measure of success, and many coaches focus on the need for a 100 percent effort (attitude) from their players at all times.

If the letters in the word "attitude" are assigned a numerical ranking according to their position in the alphabet, they total 100 percent. You can create a fun exercise with your child by having her assign the numerical ranking to each letter and discovering for herself that the total is 100 percent. The message is clear: As much as anything else, it is our attitude that determines our future success.

━ ▪ ━ ▪ ━ ▪ ━ ▪ ━ ▪ ━ ▪ ━ ▪ ━ ▪ ━ ▪ ━ ▪ ━ ▪ ━ ▪ ━ ▪ ━ ▪ ━

A	01	(first letter in alphabet)
T	20	
T	20	
I	09	
T	20	
U	21	
D	04	
E	05	
	100%	

Measure Progress

If done correctly, the sports commercial your child writes will include guideposts for behavior and sought-after, measurable outcomes. If you haven't prepared a sports commercial, you and your child should substitute with a discussion that clearly reveals what each of you want to get out of sports involvement. Whether it is decided that the child should have specific goals (swim 50 meters in 1:10), general goals (to get better at basketball), or implied goals (C.J., we just want you to have fun), both the parents and players need a measuring device to determine if the resources spent on sports are producing the anticipated goals.

The time interval for measuring progress can vary greatly depending on the athlete's age, the length of the season, and nature of the goals. The interval between evaluations should be short enough so that: 1) the athlete stays motivated by frequent reports of success; 2) the family stays focused on the athletic goals; 3) the athlete feels accountable for the goals (which is how responsibility is learned); and 4) timely corrective action can be taken if the program isn't leading toward the goals stated or implied in the sports commercial.

Without a measuring device, praise is restricted to something as broad as: "Nice job!" which is not as motivational as specific reference to improvement in a skill. "Great job; your number of assists is twice as many as last week" is far more specific than a general compliment. This kind of feedback, even if it is occasionally negative, motivates a player much more than hearing a frequent "nice job" type of praise.

Some parents feel that establishing basic measuring tools is a bad idea because it seems to put too much pressure on a child. Starting too soon will overemphasize competitiveness and add unwanted stress; however, starting too late delays learning personal accountability.

We believe parents should find a way to monitor progress which is not threatening to the child. But they must realize that their children will have to measure up to standards many times over in life. Sports offers the social matrix within which a youngster may learn to confidently withstand an evaluation.

As the following story demonstrates, the timing and manner of delivering an evaluation can have serious impact on its effectiveness.

A player had just finished a crucial game in which the team qualified for the league championships — a fantastic experience for him and his teammates. They had lost most of their games in earlier years, but as a result of hard work from the players and positive help from parents, they were now witnessing the translation of personal improvement into team success. One player, however, probably turned in the worst game of his high school career, yet his team rose to the occasion and compensated for his shortcomings. The coach congratulated everyone for great team play and rescuing a win when it looked as if they would lose. While disappointed at his performance, the single player took great satisfaction in the knowledge that he had been a major factor in the team's success all season long and, without him, there would not have been a playoff game. His good feeling disappeared, however, even before he got on the team bus because his father stopped him in the parking lot. There the parent harangued the boy, pointing out all of his mental and physical errors and how he nearly lost the game for his team.

What the father meant to have a positive effect turned out to be demeaning for his son. He neglected to open his critique with anything positive or with congratulations for the team's success. It would have been a good idea to first ask the boy how he felt about his game and to develop a post-game conversation in a more relaxed atmosphere.

Building Measuring Yardsticks
Into Skill-Building Drills

Players at any age and in any organized program will want to know if they are improving. It is best if they can see the improvement for themselves and find reinforcement through coaches, parents, and peers. This is true for beginning and accomplished athletes. Good coaches (not just athletic coaches) create skill practices that progressively lead to noticeable improvement.

"Okay, team," the coach shouts, "last week we dribbled the ball around the gym three times without stopping; this week we're going to do it five times, and change hands at least once." Monitoring progress by parent and coach, and designing detailed ways that players can self-monitor progress, becomes more and more important as athletes become better at what they do.

▬ ▪ ▬ ▪ ▬ ▪ ▬ ▪ ▬ ▪ ▬ ▪ ▬ ▪ ▬ ▪ ▬ ▪ ▬ ▪ ▬

Families play a major role in maintaining enthusiasm for sports if they can help the athlete identify improvement. Charting skills, which can be easily recorded, provides the most graphic illustration of improvement. A handwritten chart written on a piece of school paper, similar to the example below, and posted in the athlete's room will keep the focus on positive improvements. (A family reminder: It's important to tell your children about the improvements you notice in their sense of responsibility, attitude, and other intrinsic outcomes as well.)

Activity	*Number Performed*	*Performance Goal*
1. Sit-ups in one minute	13 (1 Feb.)	25
	16 (12 Feb.)	
	22 (27 Feb.)	
	30 (1 Apr.)	35
	37 (15 Apr.)	40
	43 (27 Apr.)	50
2. Free-throws	2 (1 Nov.)	3 of 10
	3 (8 Nov.)	5 of 10
	4 (15 Nov.)	
	3 (22 Nov.)	
	5 (29 Nov.)	
	6 (6 Dec.)	8 of 10

Evaluate Results

The purpose of a sports program evaluation is to make improvements for future participants, to learn how the family can make better choices in the future, and to be able to adjust a current program as it unfolds. Evaluation is a continual process that begins with the first interaction with the program. Parents should focus their evaluations on the positive aspects of the program, as well as those aspects that could be improved. The sample evaluation form we've printed on page 175 gives you an idea of the things you should be looking for as the season progresses.

The section of this chapter just concluded, Measuring Progress, described how to evaluate a sports program against the goals or objectives set forth in the sports commercial. Without wanting to sound negative, this current section alerts parents to early warning signs that their intervention is needed. One of the values of measuring progress is to judge when it becomes necessary for parents to intervene because the program may be disappointing to the players.

There is one overriding reason why young people quit sports: they are not receiving the positive experiences they anticipated. Aware parents can read the signs and prevent the deterioration of interest before it gets to the "I Quit" stage. All too often it is the program that is quitting the child, which ultimately leads to the youngster recognizing that he is not needed and, most offensive to him, may not be wanted.

An Evaluation of the Parents' Experiences

The family participates in youth sports, not just the young players. Parents should evaluate the sports experience from their individual viewpoints. Their evaluation can reveal ways to make the sports journey more enjoyable for the whole family, which in turn solidifies the family's commitment to and joy from youth sports involvement.

Parents stay up late at night retelling each other how Jordan swam the entire length of the pool for the first time, or that Ruthie led the girls' soccer team in a cheer for the opposing players. Experiences such as these and others are some of the ways youngsters make their parents proud. For most of these proud parents, watching their children master new emotional and physical skills of self-reliance is one of the purest joys.

The vast majority of parents report that each individual sports season was a rewarding experience for them — and for unselfish reasons. The stories about parents supposedly reliving their own youthful glory days through their children's sports accomplishments are, we feel, greatly exaggerated in number. Likewise, few parents sit in the grandstands anxiously waiting for their child to show superior athletic prowess so that they can egotistically say, "Yeah, that's my kid; he's just a chip off the old block."

It's essential to know the path the young person has chosen in order to help him get the most out of the sports experience. If there has been a marked change of attitude or disregard for the Team Family's basic sports agreement, it's time to refocus and rekindle interest. Without follow-up meetings, there is little chance of getting back on track. These evaluations need to take place soon after the season starts and continue on a regular basis. If expectations were spelled out clearly in the beginning, there is a far greater chance the whole process will work effectively.

These evaluations, which can be accurate only if the players are involved, once again provide an opportunity for sports to bring families together for meaningful discussions.

Choose an Alternate Route

If there seem to be dramatic shifts away from original progress agreements, don't take it as a sign of defeat. Locating an alternate sports program which may be more suitable will allow the child to learn the lessons sports has to offer. On the other hand, if there is a lack of interest on the child's part there will be ample time to find other just as satisfying non-sport activities which will have their own unique value systems. In any event, spotting the problem early gives the young person time to discover positive benefits from an alternate use of their free time.

Sportsmanship:
Bringing Out the Best Behavior

Examples of good sportsmanship abound at all levels of sport. A football lineman pulls the quarterback he just sacked back to his feet. A coach asks the umpires if the start of the game can be delayed ten minutes because the opposing team arrived late and hasn't had time for sufficient warm-up. Many parents cheer for players on both teams when they make a good play. Good sportsmanship is still the norm in youth sports. But there is ample room for improvement.

During the TV coverage of the World Little League Championships, Americans were impressed to see the Taiwanese (a country frequently playing in the championships) Little League players politely bow to the umpire if they are called out on strikes. In the U.S., a player can get away with glowering at the umpire, and parents can occasionally be heard calling the umpire, or opposing players,

derogatory names. If parent modeling of poor sportsmanship is allowed to exist, it's only a matter of time before
youngsters use disparaging words.

The best way to teach good sportsmanship is for
parents and coaches to model it. Children learn good sportsmanship from adults. When we encourage youth to be good
sports, we are asking them to abide by the following four
tests of good sportsmanship:
1. Do I abide by the rules of the contest?
2. Am I respectful and courteous to everyone involved
   in the contest?
3. Do I display emotional control?
4. Do I understand that sports is just a part of life and
   not life itself?

By upholding good sportsmanship, we are building
into young athletes the same values and behavior that they
will need to be successful parents, business professionals
and civic leaders.

Too often we have heard that the emotional nature of
sports and the physical combativeness make it impossible
for young athletes to be consistently sportsmanlike. Young
players will make sportsmanship mistakes that we can
accept; but we can't accept as fact that the nature of certain
sports prohibits civil behavior. Be highly suspect of any
behavior committed in the name of sports which is not
acceptable off the field.

So, as a parent, what level of sportsmanship should be
expected from your young athlete? We believe that you must
expect the absolute highest and model it yourself consistently. Parents and coaches should set the highest standards,
explain those standards, and hold the players to them.

Don't succumb to the poor sportsmanship examples
that permeate all levels of sport. Explain to your players that

someone else doing something wrong is not a license to repeat similar behavior. It is a hollow win when it is achieved by dirty and unfair play.

Behaviors we would especially like to see eradicated from sports include:

1. Demeaning remarks from the fans. Think about it: how can a child not be adversely affected when an adult calls her a hurtful name? The civil law, "If you don't have something nice to say, don't say anything" applies to sports also.

2. Intentional violation of the rules. Play by the spirit of the rules as well as the letter of the rules.

3. Down-talking the opponents before or after the game. Putting other people down is no way to lift ourselves up.

4. Derision of the umpires. It is human to "see" what we want to have happen. Umpires try to see objectively, but partisans want to see positive outcomes for their cause. A bias to one side distorts what we see. Trust the umpires' objectivity and forgive them their mistakes, which are inevitable.

5. Excessive physical aggression. The desire to tackle someone is different than the desire to hurt them in the process. The desire to play better than someone is different than the desire to belittle them in the process.

6. Finding fault or not accepting responsibility for one's own shortcomings. Accepting responsibility is so elemental to all human growth — the people who learn this early in life are fortunate.

Your opponent in sports is a standard against which you test your skills. He is not an enemy. To oppose someone does not require that you dislike him.

We cannot overemphasize that our incentive in writing this book is to bring high moral values back to youth sports. Maybe we can't change the mores of the current generation of adult athletes, but we all share the responsibility for changing the future by what we tolerate in today's youth sports programs.

The Cost of Playing: Money and Time

One of the most important factors in selecting a sport and level of play is the financial consideration. Children from families with very restricted means have made it to the top of every sport, but in general, the more competitive the program, the greater the affiliated costs in terms of both money and time. Many non-school sport activities have training camps, weekend meetings, seminars and special travel requirements associated with them. School-based teams also make additional sports activities available. These include confidence-building camps, group weight lifting, and strategy sessions. Often these camps are organized and supervised by school varsity coaches or college coaches. The vast majority are excellent — and well-attended by the more serious athletes — and they provide a level of instruction that is not available in the traditional school program.

The world is literally unlimited for youth sports — both school and non-school teams have played in foreign competitions. Families hire individual trainers (even for pre-teens) and year-round training is the norm in an increasing number of sports. All the extras create expenses, and families need to set their limit. The costs of the essentials creep up in a hurry. Know the cost of the following:

Footwear ($60 - $150)

Uniforms (some sports require four or five changes of uniform) ($40 - $200)

Medical insurance and physical exams ($10 - $50)

Membership fees ($5 - $100)

Pro-rata share of gym rentals, equipment, and offici-ating fees ($2 - $15)

Protective equipment ($50 - $250)

Travel, rooms and meals ($80 - $300)

Warm-ups ($40 - $150)

Educational materials ($5 - $25)

School athletic budgets cover some of these costs, and certain community-based programs provide scholarships and other means of financial assistance.

If finances are going to create hardships, parents are faced with the options of working within organizations to initiate fund-raising activities or telling their child that he will not participate. (In our experience, fund-raising builds team spirit and is an integral part of many sports programs.) There are programs which may not have the desired level of competition, but they do have excellent volunteer coaches and low expenses. Determined athletes and parents can usually find a way to participate in organized sports.

The additional expense for young people in sports has been criticized by many as going beyond the purpose of sport as a learning tool. Others consider the extra cost to be reasonable for a second helping of self-confidence, positive attitudes, teamwork, and the lifelong values learned in sports. Even those critical of the extra sports instruction and expense often approve of private instruction and camps in music, drama or computer technology. (Yes, there are computer summer camps!) If you are confident that advanced training will benefit your child, investigating all the options will improve the financial and investment decision.

Thirty-three thousand dollars was raised by a twelve-member youth all-star basketball team, plus two coaches, to travel for two weeks in Australia and New Zealand. They played five games: that's $6,600 per game! Each team member received $200 for souvenir money. The trip was educationally valuable and a terrific experience for fourteen people. The next year the school program eliminated seven basketball squads due to levy failures, and 105 (7 times 15) young players missed an opportunity to play in 140 games. Thirty thousand dollars would have prevented the program cuts, paid travel, coaching, officiating, facility use, and gymnasium utilities for the season. That's only $215 per game.

In another case, to enhance scholarship chances, a single parent withdrew $7,000 from the "family college education savings account" to send her graduating daughter to Europe on a sixteen-day sports team tour. The daughter chose to delay college enrollment one year while she got a job and replenished the education account. Her European trip was fun, and she eventually graduated from college. This family employed a good strategy.

Team Family should consider all options and alternatives for achieving skill and attitude objectives during the off-season. Some examples that reduce costs yet reach the "improvement" objective for the youngster:

- Join a local summer team/league.
- Substitute conditioning camps for sports camps.
- Check libraries/schools for self-development programs (sports-specific videos and books).
- Work at the camp to offset costs.
- Secure group/team rates.

- Use different sports to enhance transferable skills (example: improve foot speed).
- Attend half-sessions at camps.
- Hold your own "Family Camp"; obtain objectives from the coach and work on skills at home.

When Are You Paying Too Much?

Many sincere educators believe an over-emphasis on sports has a negative impact on the child who has paid all the dues and yet has experienced an inequity of benefits. Some young athletes who dutifully attend summer camps never make a school team, although that was the player's sole purpose for attending camp. These educators correctly point out that:

1. Even if a marginally gifted youngster does make the school team, it takes a big investment for the precious few minutes of playing time because there aren't enough minutes of playing time to satisfy everyone;

2. Coaches encourage everyone to attend extra camps and forgo other summer activities, knowing full well that many will not reap the rewards for their time and effort;

3. Family activities (weddings, visits to grandparents, birthday celebrations) now compete with sports obligations, resulting in family strife.

Camps can run from one day to an entire summer, and cost as little as nothing to as much as many thousands of dollars. If the goal is to excel in individual sports such as tennis, gymnastics or skiing, be prepared to attend training camps with the best U.S. coaches. This could entail trips to Florida, Colorado, or even Europe, with $100-per-day camp fees. Costs for the more typical single-session and popular two-day camps have a wide fee range, depending on location and the reputation of the coach. "You get what you pay for" is also applicable to sports.

These are all excellent reasons for careful deliberation before you choose the level of dedication to a program. Investigate the total costs before committing. Don't hesitate to make phone calls and compare costs. Check the sponsoring organization thoroughly before writing the check.

There are two certainties: the price is too high if 1) the player doesn't enjoy the extra time in sport; and 2) she isn't receiving the benefits that were expected. Be watchful for the child's distress signals, which are listed in the following section on burnout.

Athletic Burnout: The Flame Dies Down

Everybody has occasionally experienced the blahs — that emotional and physical state where it is hard to get ourselves going: work isn't appealing, school isn't stimulating, or our relationships aren't exciting. The catch-all term used to describe this loss of interest in an activity is "burnout." There are two very basic, underlying causes of burnout which hold true whether talking about kids, adults, sports, business or marriages.

First, we experience burnout because the rewards for continuing are no longer perceived as being worth the sacrifices. The rewards are too small or the sacrifices too great. Second, we become burned out when we perceive that the chances of being successful, i.e., of receiving the rewards, are very slim. Most people are willing to work hard for something of value if they believe their efforts will hit paydirt.

Alert parents and coaches are able to spot the symptoms of youth burnout and prevent the deterioration of interest from reaching the "I quit" stage. Burnout is preventable, and it is frequently not caused by factors under a young athlete's control. If the causes of burnout are treated instead of the symptoms, the enthusiasm for sports can be recovered. Let's look first at the symptoms; then the causes behind the symptoms; and finally, how to treat the causes.

Symptoms of Burnout

The following signals are strong indications that your athlete is falling out of interest with sports:

- The athlete stops talking about sports to the family.
- The child needs a push to get to practice on time.
- There is less socializing with other members of the team.
- An increase in negative self-talk about sports: "I can't" is heard more often than "I can."
- Little self-improvement is made at practice.
- Increased negative comments about the program and external factors, such as fellow teammates, coaches, rules, competitors.
- Pre-competition excitement has vanished.

Six Causes of Burnout

1. Lack of real success. Success reveals the value of a coach who can impart athletic skills and winning attitudes and the importance of setting clear, achievable and measurable goals. Reaching goals allow an athlete to see that he has made progress and therefore experience success. Even

at a young age people want to know that their time investment is producing positive results. A word of caution: yes,
it is necessary to pass out praise often for meaningful
successes, but giving insincere praise or being patronizing
to young athletes is recognized by them and is a turn-off to
sports. It's a fine line between praising and patronizing.
Patronizing athletes makes them question themselves and
their success.

2. Excessive pressure to perform well, win, or meet
sports demands.

Consider these subtle pre-teen pressures:

Fathers at a Game:
First Father: "That is my son who just passed the ball
to your son, who scored. He shoots very well."
Second Father: "Yeah, like his dad. I expect him to do
as well as I did."

Daughter to Mother:
Daughter: "Mom, the coach wants me to go to
summer camp."
Mother: "You will miss going on vacation and visiting
Grandmother."
Daughter: "But I won't make the team if I don't go to
camp."
Mother: "Who told you that?"
Daughter: "Janice didn't go to camp, and she was cut
last year."
Mother: "I will call your coach."
Daughter: "Oh please don't do that; she will think I
don't want to go."

Son to Father During Breakfast:

Son: "If I go to practice, my homework will be late. If I miss practice, I won't start against Kennydale."

Father: "Why didn't you do your homework last night instead of going to Sharon's birthday party?"

Son: "Dad, everybody goes to Sharon's parties. Maybe I'll call Kyla and copy her homework."

Father: "No, that's cheating! You have to make a choice. Homework or practice. Your homework is more important."

Son: "NOT TO ME IT ISN'T! I have practiced for two years to start against Kennydale. I'm going to practice!"

Father: "I'm going to call your coach; this is ridiculous."

Son: "Go ahead, call him."

3. The workload at practice is too much for the age group.

Sports for youth is recreation, not a profession. Tolerance to pain (and extreme fatigue is painful) is a turn-off to most young athletes.

4. Overextension in total life commitments (could be physical or emotional, and most often a combination of the two). Yes, some kids seem to thrive on a crammed schedule, but parents need to watch the barometer for overload.

5. Being blocked from spending time with valued friends.

6. The external rewards provided by the program for doing well have little value to the participants.

Robin, a sophomore, made the swimming team. Ryan, a junior wrestler, asked her to attend a movie after a swim meet. Two weeks later Robin attended her first wrestling match and joined the other girlfriends of wrestlers in a special cheering section. She recognized that she knew too little about wrestling even to cheer at the right times. Robin watched videos and read books on wrestling for the next two weeks. She eagerly awaited the next home wrestling competition and planned on attending the rest of the team's competitions. This took time away from her swim practice time.

Robin's swim coach informed her of his concern about her lack of improvement and told her he would need to move her to the JV team if she couldn't spend more pool time practicing. Robin said she understood and asked to be moved to the JVs so she would have time to do the things which interested her more.

Approval by peers, popularity and success are the three strongest social motives of youth. Sports is usually an excellent means of achieving all three, but if it becomes an inhibitor, as it did in Robin's case, a lack of interest in sports — burnout — might be noticed.

Don't assume that burnout is always a negative situation. The analysis of rewards and sacrifices might reveal that the rewards from life would increase if sports participation was scaled back a bit in time or intensity.

Treating Causes of Burnout

Temporary alternatives. Time away from a sport, with a graceful return, will usually rekindle enthusiasm. An objective from a secondary interest might be achieved; for example, completing the postponed lessons, making time to practice.

Provide opportunities to create. Offer a new and different challenge and/or responsibility.

Realistic expectations. Provide for a catharsis. Invite and accept an open discussion of "involved," "committed," "passion" and "addicted" athletes and the relationship they have to their sport. If the cause is lack of confidence in self, making and meeting realistic expectations is a remedy.

Time-out to build confidence. Arrange recovery time. Burnout is not an injury, but it can be equally debilitating. When enthusiasm diminishes at a greater-than-normal rate, dissatisfaction with performance is usually a symptom. Instead of increasing practices and "time on task," treat the cause: loss of enthusiasm. Diagnose the cause, offer a prescription, then give time for "enthusiasm recovery" in the same manner as one would recover from injury. Enthusiasm has been rediscovered by some youth simply by contact with their favorite high school athlete.

Fight through it. Believe burnout does not exist; don't accept it. Find a new "challenge" to become enthused about. "Beating Burnout" is a challenge some accept, especially when they know others care.

Preventing Burnout

To remedy burnout, the partnership must treat the cause(s), not the symptoms. The best way to learn the root cause is to talk with the athlete. If the cause is lack of success, then the partnership must remove the obstacle blocking success or show the player how to overcome the obstacle.

There are so many reasons that a player isn't progressing at a satisfactory rate. Unfortunately, the misguided remedy of merely exhorting the child to put out more, which is an example of treating the symptom, is frequently the parents' or coach's choice of intervention.

Treatment of burnout, which involves action on the part of each partner, would include:

1. Remind the player of the progress he has made. Seeing success is an intrinsic (internal) reward. This reinforces the principle that athletic skills, which can be measurable, need to be built into a youth sports program. As a family, frequently relive the great play or special moments experienced in sports

2. Organize more than one social function for the team during the season. Going for a pizza, as a team, after games or practice is a reward and is often seen as an effort to bring an element of fun to the team.

3. Make the travel trips to away games pleasure trips. Stop at aquariums, mini-golf, or other youth attractions.

4. Be a captive and attentive audience for adolescents. Listen to them! Get their ideas on how to improve attitudes.

5. Encourage parents to compliment players other than their own.

6. Arrange to have an inspirational celebrity or a former team member visit the team.

7. Ask the local sports radio station to do a brief interview with players who are positive influences in ways other than outstanding performance.

8. Submit an article to your local sportswriter about a player's positive influence.

Remember this axiom about motivation: The same reward, furnished over and over again, begins to lose its value. Verbiage such as "you did a great job today" sends young athletes on an emotional high when heard for the first time, but not when the same phrase is used repetitively.

The opposite is true for sacrifices. The same sacrifice, experienced repeatedly, grows as a de-motivator. Skipping one party with friends shouldn't be a motivational downer for kids, but being prevented repetitively from sharing special moments with friends will become so.

When asked what changes would entice them to return to the sport, boys' and girls' responses differed only slightly:

"I would play again if...

BOYS	GIRLS
1. Practices were more fun	1. Practices were more fun
2. I could play more	2. No conflict with studies
3. Coaches understood players	3. Coaches understood players
4. No conflict with studies	4. No social life conflicts
5. Coaches taught better	5. I could play more
6. No social life conflicts	6. Coaches taught better

In conclusion, don't dismiss burnout as just a cycle that everyone goes through. Get past the symptoms, ferret out the causes, and either redesign an involvement that fits the child's expectations and needs, or overhaul the current rewards and sacrifices so that sports participation becomes fun again.

Igniter Phrases

"Igniter phrases" have been proven to have greater motivation impact than constructive criticism. (Constructive criticism is necessary, and a good motivator uses a mix of igniter phrases, specific constructive criticism, and specific praise.) Young athletes contend they are encouraged or discouraged by words parents use to express approval or disapproval. Common "encouragers" from the kids' list are:

That's good!	I like that!
Great idea.	You can do it.
Do that again!	Let's go!
That's a winner.	Go ahead...try it.
You're hot.	Fantastic!

Keep going!   Can you teach me?
I'm proud of you.   Wow! Let's start a new trend.

Discipline

Sports has long been thought of as the learning ground where young people acquire discipline. The purpose of sports is certainly not to instill discipline, but it is true that sports provides excellent learning opportunities to develop self-discipline. Discipline has two meanings, both of which will surface in sports.

First, discipline is a personality characteristic meaning self-imposed restraint. It takes discipline to maintain emotional control when something unpleasant or undeserved happens. For example, if an opposing player fouls your young son, as a parent you hope your child has the discipline to maintain mental composure. Similarly, it takes discipline to go to soccer practice every day after it has been rainy and cold for an entire week. Discipline, as a favorable trait, is akin to determination and self-control. We expect the coach to instill discipline; and we trust that the coach knows how to do that in a non-abusive manner.

Second, discipline is the consequence of violating an expected standard of behavior. Athletes who skip practice because it was too cold could face disciplinary action ranging from a reprimand, a penalty of cleaning the field after a game, or being benched during the next game. Discipline in this sense does not have a favorable connotation.

Parents have a right, and obligation, to know the coach's philosophy about and method of implementing discipline. It is one of the topics that needs to be discussed during the pre-season meeting with coaches and parents.

Good coaches apply discipline in a consistent manner to all offenders of the rules, which could make it difficult, if not impossible, to please all parents.

If the conditions for which discipline will be applied and the severity of it are announced and discussed prior to its use, then parents and players are at least prepared for its physical and emotional impact. It is idealistic to think that the issue of discipline won't arise.

Discipline should not be dished out to relieve the anger of the offended. Rather, it is used as the best means of altering an undesirable behavior.

Discipline is typically meted out for intentional violation of team rules, and for intentional or unintentional violation of the game rules. It is generally inappropriate to impose disciplinary action for the following situations:

1. As a means of correcting a lack of talent.
2. As a means of correcting behavior that has not been previously disallowed.
3. As blanket discipline to apply to a group when not everyone in the group is an offender.
4. As a means of correcting a no-fault accident.

Discipline should be applied sparingly and firmly. If there is a spate of disciplinary actions, then the coaching staff is failing in its teaching function. Sports is recreation (fun), and a high incidence of discipline takes the fun out of sport.

The Specialization Dilemma

One of the most controversial sports debates centers around whether young athletes should participate in only one sport and, if so, when does specialization begin? Both authors strongly agree that there is much more to be gained by sampling a variety of sports prior to entering high school.

We have heard most of the justifications given supporting specialization prior to this age (my child won't be successful in high school sports if he doesn't focus now; my daughter was born with a dream to be an Olympian, and in her sport you have to start young; all Jimmy wants to do is play soccer, why should he try something else; our whole family competes in tennis year round, it's our family thing) and we still urge parents of below-14-year-olds to explore different sports.

To specialize or not is ultimately a family decision and should be decided in a family setting. There are always exceptions when dealing with human issues, and if one family decides that specialization is right for them, and they have investigated all the pros and cons, we're not going to say they're wrong.

The decision to specialize isn't a permanent sports obligation. If other sports and learning opportunities become more attractive, give them a try.

Parents need to know the rewards their player expects to receive from specialization. The only way to know is to ask. Make sure the rewards are valid — maybe the system can't return the rewards the youth is looking for. One of the reasons young people require adult guidance is that they don't see the big picture; the child's short-term rewards — and pressures — to specialize may be incongruent with the parents' more global view.

Also, parents, if you condone or are pushing for specialization, be certain that your reasons for this position match the child's true desires and that he or she isn't following along to please you.

As we said, specialization is a controversy, and the authors have differing opinions about specialization at the high school level. Rather than present our individual differences, we collectively present the pros and cons of sport specialization for young people.

Building a case against specialization

1. Specializing in a single sport deprives youth of opportunities for a comprehensive "sports" education. Sport specialization is no more logical than advising a learner to take only math or English courses in high school because that is what they like to do or do best. Experiencing diversified opportunities, working with a variety of coaches, experimenting, transferring skills from one activity to another, and living through success and failure are the foundations of intellectual and social growth. The primary purpose of youth sports is to be a laboratory of life.

2. It is not the athlete, but the sport, that benefits from specialization. The best athletes are actively recruited and given special attention so that they will stay with one sport. The real bottom line is victories for the team. Here we have youth serving sport, the opposite of what is right: sport serving youth.

3. A tenacious, hard-training young athlete actually may be more talented in a sport other than what she is specializing in, but she might never get a chance to discover this. The distance runner, running in part because his dad was a track star in college, may not have inherited the same genetic traits that made his dad great. No amount of work will return the success in running that the child deserves from his effort. However, the same boy could be a dolphin in the water.

4. A player may become better in one sport from what they learn in another. For example, football running backs

can learn to sprint during track season. A study of the degree of specialization by graduating high school football players selected to participate in state all-star games showed 100 percent to be multi-sport participants.

5. Specialization at the highest levels of competition conflicts with other obligations and opportunities youth have. Some off-season youth sports teams play as many as forty games — and this is called the off-season. There is never a family season, when family activities truly come first.

6. Young athletes have no time to recover physically or mentally when there is no off-season. The school coach has to produce a winning season in a short period of time with the athletes, and then the select team coach has to do the same. The intensity is always too high.

7. Specialization typically involves teams that travel and play a lot of tournaments. This becomes expensive, especially if coaching fees and yet one more uniform are added to the costs.

Building a case in favor of specialization
1. What specialization lacks in breadth of learning experiences, it more than makes up for in depth of learning. As young players further and further refine the mental and physical aspects of a sport, they are exposed to the finer intricacies and advanced techniques of the game. Young athletes, if they are to excel in one sport, must be on the accelerated learning curve.

By working with the same athlete for a longer period of time, the coaches better understand the child and can create learning opportunities that are individualized. The coach/athlete relationship is stronger, and this relationship can have a very positive effect on the child.

2. The choice to specialize leaves room for the parents and young players to select programs and coaches that model the values they admire. "Specialized" programs can be just as concerned about total person development as any other sports opportunity.

3. The decision to specialize is always temporary and is only in place as long as the young player is having fun and meeting success. Specialization is a system that allows youngsters to stay involved in an activity they enjoy most.

4. Specialization offers young athletes more time to be involved in sports. They can practice and compete on a year-round basis, which gives them more time to soak up the benefits of sports. It's nice to think that young people would be hanging out with the family when not playing sports, but that isn't usually the case. They are with their peers doing other things — things not always as beneficial as sports.

Athletes who specialize, while not involved in as many sporting activities, do participate in as many non-sport activities and have grade point averages as high as those who don't specialize. The choice to specialize does not create any characteristic deficiencies that behavioral studies have identified.

5. Pursuing an interest in a single sport is no more exhausting for a player than jumping from one sport to the next. Most specialized athletes, in fact, don't play year round — in most areas there is no opportunity to play baseball, for example, during the winter months.

6. Specialization can be, but does not have to be, expensive. It is the upper echelons of competition that tend to be expensive — not all programs aspire to compete at this level. Buying the necessary equipment to compete in three sports can be equally expensive.

As a final note, it should be mentioned that some athletes do both: that is, they specialize and experience a variety of sports at the same time. They have decided to be their best in just one sport, and in that sport they practice and compete with a greater determination and focus. During another season of the year they could be playing volleyball at a much lesser intensity.

9

Parenting the Gifted Athlete

■ — ■ — ■ — ■ — ■ — ■ — ■ — ■ — ■ — ■ — ■ — ■ —

This chapter discusses the special circumstances that might arise in families which include a gifted athlete. "Gifted" is described as those athletes who have the talent (whether it is derived from special physical capabilities or from mental skills such as tenacity and a "sixth sense" to understand the game) to consistently perform at higher levels than their peers. With their special gifts, these athletes can become standout varsity players in high school or go on to play in college. Gifted, as used in this chapter, does not designate only those who could play in the NBA or set records at the Olympics. There are a lot of gifted athletes; whether they choose to exploit their gift is a matter of choice.

For the vast majority of youth participating in sports, reaching the status of elite athlete is either not important or is unattainable due to conditions beyond their control (time, money, opportunity, talent). The rewards and lifelong lessons of those who choose to "participate" are equal to, and often greater than, those who choose to excel. The lessons of determination and mental preparation, as presented in this chapter, pertain to far more than just sports and are recommended for parents of children who are gifted in some aspect (which is virtually every child).

Is My Child One of the Few
Who Could Excel in Sports?

This is the question that might occur to parents whose children perform well in sports. With all the adulation afforded super-star athletes, it's quite natural that some youngsters want to grow up and be like their heroes. But is it realistic? Can juvenile fantasy be converted into the young adult determination required to excel in sports? Are more kids helped or harmed by aspiring to be a champion? These are questions parents have to answer, and there will be many tough decisions to make before a child should be launched on the road to becoming a nationally known athlete.

It could be that your child's special gift is more germane to non-sporting activities. Children have hidden talents. He or she may be especially creative, artistic, inno-vative, mentally quick, or possess any number of traits that mark a gifted person. Parents want to look at all sides of this question, to include asking: "Is this talent or gift applicable to sports only?"

There is no hard-and-fast rule or standardized test that reveals to parents whether or not their child has champi-onship ability. For athletes under fourteen years of age, the best criteria for assessing a child's physical aptitude are subjective. If unbiased coaches, parents and other players frequently praise your child's skills, then he or she may have the potential of a gifted athlete. Being a gifted athlete is in part a natural gift, but to a greater extent it is finding the sport one is best suited for and then coupling that with hard work and a positive attitude. Exceptional athletes are usually those who learned the real value of work ethics.

At some point in a young athlete's development, if she wants to be a champion, her decision to work harder and smarter than age-group peers will have to be made. There are two important considerations associated with the decision to work harder and smarter. The first one is: will the rewards earned be worth the extra effort? And second, will the athlete enjoy a more competitive sports environment? No situation justifies an athlete's pursuit of the status and benefits of becoming a champion if the process is not enjoyable. There are too many champions who have made it to the top — with regret that they traded years of their life for the brief satisfaction of being admired for something that they didn't enjoy doing.

The best way to groom a future champion is to provide a supportive athletic environment which implants a fervent enjoyment of sports in the child. This enjoyment, if nurtured and guided, can become a healthy passion for sports. We recommend that you allow your athletic child the opportunity to participate in many sports. By trying a variety of sports, by the process of natural selection, children usually end up in the sport best suited for them.

If a child is passionate about his sport, he may begin to follow the pathway of champions as early as age six. This is especially true for the extremely competitive individual sports such as swimming, gymnastics and skiing. We urge extreme caution as well as objective input from highly skilled professional advisors/sports psychologists before starting kids on this fast track at this early age! There is a great possibility of making serious errors of judgment if kids are pushed too far too soon. A devotion to football, baseball or basketball need not be developed so early. The gifted athlete who does not focus on a particular sport early is not necessarily at a disadvantage. There are Olympians who did not choose their sport until they were in their twenties. They were good athletes first; they specialized second.

Specificity

Specificity is the magic word for athletic success. Sprinters must sprint, swimmers must swim, and tennis players have to play the game if they want to become great at what they do. The body adapts to the specific physical workload to which it is subjected. No amount of swimming will make a gifted athlete a great tennis player.

Encouragement, Not Coercion

Aside from consistent training for a specific sport, athletes also need constant encouragement. However, in sports, there is a fine line between encouragement and coercion. When Dad accompanies his teenage daughter on a training run and suggests to her that she should be able to stay up with her forty-plus-year-old dad, is the message encouragement or coercion? Depending on how it is delivered, it easily could be coercion. As parents of successful athletes have informed us, effective strategy for encouragement is simply to "Put opportunities in front of the child, build in fun along each step, and take an active interest in your child's athletic adventures."

How Much Training?

How much training a young athlete can handle is a controversial subject and varies from sport to sport. The Eastern Bloc nations (including China with its women's swimming and running programs) gained notoriety and many Olympic medals during the 1980s. Child prodigies such as Olga Korbut and Nadia Comaneci became the darlings of the world. These nations attributed their success to placing gifted children — after elaborate testing to determine the most suited sport — into national academies that demanded rigorous training under the ever-present eyes of coaches.

Under the sports programs sponsored by the Eastern Bloc nations, large national pools of potential champions were collected, and the athletes were subjected to the highest limits of physical training. Even among the best, only a few could survive the physical and emotional demands. The survivors became champions. In our Western culture, it is not acceptable to push kids as hard as some Eastern European nations do at early ages. We oppose this type of training; too many young people lose their childhood in an adult's pursuit of glory.

If parents are not familiar with recommended training regimens for specific sports and age groups, they rely on the coach to provide this information. Overtraining, especially for youth, is far worse than undertraining. For the purposes of this book, we've chosen to list the four conditions that are indications of overtraining for every sport. The overtraining signals are:

1. Depleted mental enthusiasm.
2. Chronic fatigue. The player cannot physically recover from and adapt to the training load.

3. Improvement in other areas of development begins
   to slide.
4. The family's time, patience and financial resources
   are exhausted.

An hour a day of running would probably signify
overtraining conditions for ages below thirteen. In comparison, three hours of figure skating, for the right youngster,
could easily fit within training conditions.

Good coaches, knowing how much training is needed
in each sport to reach graduated levels of performance, can
help the player and parents decide if the investment is worth
the benefits. Coaches might be biased in believing the
rewards are greater than the value attached to them by the
parents, but good coaches do not inflate the rewards to
recruit a gifted athlete. If coaches promise athletic scholarships to college, ask them to show you the actual percentages of those who have tried and been awarded scholarships. There can be no guarantees. Be cautious of anyone
who offers you a guarantee.

The national governing bodies of the individual
Olympic sports are valuable sources of information to
determine how to encourage the gifted athlete. Some
publish pamphlets which show how much different
Olympians trained during their lives and also how much
training the national team coaching staff recommends for
young athletes who have the desire to go for the gold. To
contact these national governing bodies, call the U.S.
Olympic Committee at 719-632-5551.

The best rule to remember is that it's better for parents
to push too little than too hard. Remember, the coach is
pushing a vested interest also, as might be the fans and other
teammates.

Gifted But Unmotivated Athletes

Everyone is motivated — all the time. Try to get a sleeping person out of the hammock and you might discover that he is very motivated to stay right where he is. Unmotivated merely means the individual is not fascinated enough with the challenge to change his present way of behaving. It is very easy to understand why a person may not be motivated to change. The reward to change, as perceived by the individual, may not be greater than the reward to continue as is. If you want your gifted athlete to be more highly motivated, your best (and perhaps only) way to facilitate the change is to increase her rewards to train harder and more effectively. Some parents, in an effort to motivate, offer monetary rewards to young athletes. We do not recommend this approach. Better to reward them with praise, encouragement and support, which exist in limitless supply.

If the appropriate rewards are apparent, the gifted athlete will increase his effort to live up to his ability. If the rewards are absent, so will be the desired behavior. In theory, it is just that simple. Putting the theory into practice is more difficult and, sometimes, frustrating. It requires that parents clearly understand the factors that motivate their athlete, or fail to. Also, it is important to accept the possibility that an unmotivated player may be right. Perhaps the rewards that would elicit a supreme effort do not exist. If the attraction is greater for the athlete to become a pilot, scientist, farmer or engineer, then it is right for him to spend free time engaging in activities that lead to those careers.

An effort to "light the fire" under a gifted athlete begins with a discussion about why he or she prefers the rewards that evoke the current level of commitment and what increased rewards it would take to make a greater effort appear attractive. Be careful about attaching your values to the athlete's rewards. Be careful also when lighting the fire: fires can be burned out if not refueled with praise and rewards. To help recognize what rekindles the fire, review "Why Young People Participate" in Chapter One.

Also, you should realize that there are gifted athletes who are unmotivated to excel because excellence has never been expected of them. They have learned that a minimal effort gets an acceptable outcome. They need a greater challenge. Is your child one of these?

What is Required When Choosing to Excel?

Before age twelve, serious competitors can meet all their athletic obligations and still partake in a full variety of life's other offerings. As their bodies become stronger and their minds more capable of learning, they can, and in order to win at the top level, must, put more time into sports. Sooner or later, the young athlete will have to choose between sports practice and another enjoyable activity. Only so much sleep can be sacrificed; after reaching that physical limit, time at the movies, parties or just loafing have to be restructured. Elite swimmers in high school learn how to manage time — and make sacrifices. "Double-days" are common, which means getting up around 5:00 a.m., jumping in the pool at 5:30, and swimming for an hour before breakfast and school. After school they double back for more time in the pool. This kind of persistence represents the dues one has to pay to win at the state level.

It makes very little difference if a swimmer skips one practice or competition to attend a wedding. Occasionally, even the best sleep through a morning training session. But if the missed sessions increase, so will the time it takes to swim one hundred meters. It becomes a choice: go to practice and receive the delayed rewards of improved swimming times, or attend the social activities and receive the immediate benefits of socialization. It's not a choice of right or wrong; it's a choice of preferences: "Do I want to be a champion?" Even if obtainable, it is not the right choice for everyone. This choice is also evident in the workplace. Deciding whether to spend more time with family or at one's job is a conscious decision. We can't emphasize often enough that few will reach and perform consistently well at high levels; for this reason it's crucial to evaluate athletic success with family and lifelong values!

The Hidden Rewards

Choosing to persevere today in order to collect benefits tomorrow is a lesson of tremendous importance athletes must learn. Even though dedicated athletes have more demands on their time, they still do better academically because they have learned to do their work systematically. Such systems become ingrained in the champion and stand him in good stead throughout life. The intangibles, however, such as personal growth, are not the strongest motivators for youngsters. They want immediate recognition for success, and they want tangible rewards. Tangible rewards include trophies, trips to out-of-area competitions, team jackets, new athletic equipment, and association with champions from the tier above them.

Instilling Positive Expectations

There is no greater determinant of success than belief in oneself. The greatest athletic gift you can give your children is the confidence you have in them that, despite all odds and difficulties, they will succeed. It's not whether you get knocked down in sports that matters, it's whether you get back up. By reinforcing your children's personal belief in themselves and a positive outcome, you are giving them the extra confidence that, no matter how long it takes, they will win. That's the best "pick-me-up" known to humankind. This is true for adults faced with setbacks at work or in their families. The ability to bounce back is often the difference between self-satisfaction and poor self-image.

When communicating with young people about sports, the words we say are important because they create pictures in youngster's minds. Young athletes don't internalize words: they convert words to mental pictures and then see themselves living up to the expectations of the pictures. If the coach or parent asks a child, "Why are you such a klutz?" the child develops the self-image of being a klutz. Performance is always consistent with our self-image. During the formative years, the self-image is very impressionable. The thoughts you place in the mind of a young person should always be those you fervently believe are worthy of guiding their lives. You can demonstrate the right sports techniques to a gifted athlete, you can buy her the latest equipment, you can coach her after practice, but of greater benefit, you can imbue her with self-belief. Faith in oneself moves mountains.

When you praise a young player, choose words that build a mental picture of the performance you want from him in the future. A ski coach we talked to learned this lesson in the most graphic form. At the national championships, one of his athletes skied past him in a cross-country ski race and looked stiff and tense due to the stress of being in the national championships for the first time. The coach hollered out, "Relax, you look stiff and choppy."

Nothing happened! If anything, the athlete became even more rigid and energy-wasting. Unwittingly, the coach planted the picture of a tense skier in the athlete's mind — and he enacted the picture, to the chagrin of the coach. Then, for reasons unexplainable to the coach, he created a new picture for his athlete by yelling, "Now you're looking good; keep up those long strides!" Immediately after hearing the new message, the skier changed his technique and went on to have a great race.

Parents and coaches should ever be mindful of the self-image pictures they load into the minds of unsuspecting youngsters. This is why good coaches always mention something the athlete is doing well first, then critique the actions they want the athlete to alter, and finish the instruction with a positive comment.

Here's an example of a wise coach talking: "You're doing a great job dribbling the ball up-court. Now I want you to stop dribbling and pass the ball as soon as you get into heavy traffic. If you get the ball back, go ahead and shoot; you're shooting really well tonight."

What message did the coach deliver? He planted three thoughts in the mind of the athlete: 1) The player dribbled well; 2) She needed to pass the ball; and 3) She is a good shot. Even though the athlete was corrected, her self-image was embellished during the transaction. Parents should look for opportunities to develop self-confidence in their son/daughter by using positive igniter phrases (see page 207).

Well-timed praise is a boost to the self-image — the exact place an athlete needs it. Don't allow your athlete to get down on himself after a mistake. The more times he relives a mistake in his mind, the greater the likelihood of him repeating it. An axiom in life is that our physical actions are a reflection of our mental thoughts. Use words that imbed positive pictures, and eliminate negative self-talk by your young athlete. You need to take this one step further: protect your player from negative input from other players or adults. Cutting other people down, even if they are your opponents in sports, is unsportsman-like. Your opponents in sports are your allies in life; don't tear them down — you may need them later.

Self-Responsibility is a Championship Trait

If you want young athletes to be winners, teach them to be responsible for their outcomes. Coaches don't win or lose games, nor do parents; the players do. If players habitually look elsewhere to change a poor performance, and not at themselves, they often fail to see the root cause of most shortcomings. As athletes mature and become more and more capable of accepting responsibility, give it to them. No one is going to hold their hand in later life. At some point we have to quit relying on the coach to pull us through.

The following story demonstrates a high degree of self-responsibility by the athlete (the names have been changed to protect the famous). A world champion was sitting in his room looking at a three-by-five card when his coach walked in and asked what he was doing. The athlete responded, "I'm studying a list of all the things that could go wrong and preparing a contingency plan for them."

The coach jokingly questioned, "Oh, am I on the list?" In dead seriousness, the athlete answered, "John, you are the first item on the list."

At that time, and today also, this athlete and the coach are great friends. But the athlete knew he was ultimately responsible and had to be prepared in case the coach made a mistake.

There is one particular area in which the athlete must never abdicate responsibility to the coach or parents. It is the area of goal-setting. Teach gifted athletes the basics of sound goal-setting and impress on them the importance of this skill if they expect to get the most from their sport. Personal goal-setting puts them in the driver's seat of their own athletic life — a place where no one else should be.

Advanced Goal-Setting

Athletic fields are fertile grounds for learning the effectiveness of setting goals and how to achieve them. Questions from the coach such as, "What's your goal for the season and how are you going to achieve it?" are frequent in sport. Coaches don't always have the time to work through goal-setting with the personal attention they would like to spend on each of their athletes. Parents should fill this gap and impart the skills of proper goal-setting. Don't let your young athlete escape the goal-setting process with a quick answer that does not reflect the planning necessary to achieve an inspiring goal. Failure to set a goal becomes a prime learning opportunity missed.

Parents, above all, if you miss all the practice sessions and many of the games, for goodness sake don't miss the endearing opportunity of showing strong interest in your child's goals and demonstrating to him or her how to realize these goals. Suggest to your child that she set SMART goals, and then stay involved with the progress she is making. Asking questions about the progress your children are making towards sports goals shows that you care and that sports is an important part of their upbringing. You also will discover that parent/child interaction around sports goals is an excellent entrée to goal-setting in more sensitive areas such as academics and social standards.

There are many goal-setting systems. We recommend one in which each goal is broken down into a set of SMART objectives. SMART is an easily remembered acronym for Specific, Measurable, Achievable, Relevant, and Timely. If a goal (through the establishment of objectives) meets these criteria, and if an effective plan of action is implemented, then the highest chance of success is assured.

As long as the objectives are being met, the young athlete is advancing toward the goal. When parents help their children formulate goals and objectives, it is important to distinguish a goal as a "target" and objectives as those actions that must be taken to hit the target. Below is an example of goal-setting through the use of objectives. We are using this music goal example to make a major point in the book: Everything we've been talking about is applicable to a much broader spectrum than just sports. (Chapter Eleven in its entirety is committed to this issue.)

Overall Goal:

To Be the Best Musician I Can Possibly Be

Most literature on athletic goal-setting states that goals should be specific and have a completion date. We feel goals for youth should be more general — encourage them to be the best that they can be and let them know they are esteemed regardless of their performance ability.

Objectives: Identify the stepping stones essential for reaching the goal.

Objective 1: To be a member of the school marching band for two years during my high school career.

Sub-objective: To maintain a 90 percent attendance at practices.

Objective 2: To be selected to first chair before I graduate.

Objective 3: To play solo during a public concert.

Objective 4: To perform at five concerts for senior citizens or similar charitable groups.

Objective 5: To complete a college correspondence course on music composition.

In the above example, the objectives written out are SMART — they provide direction and measurable criteria to evaluate progress. When an objective is achieved and new objectives put in place, the performers move closer to their ultimate goal. The objective of a runner to "be a good runner," provides direction, but not a measurable challenge, and thus the motivational aspect of the objective is diminished. However, "to run a five-kilometer race without stopping or walking" carries a measurable challenge; and to do it in less than thirty minutes adds another specific criterion of success.

You can be a super motivator by helping your son or daughter establish SMART objectives so they can be recognized for making progress toward their goals (dreams).

Specific Objectives. *An error:* "I want to be a winner." It's a nice thought, but it doesn't provide any direction or suggest what actions must be taken to achieve the goal. *The correction:* "I want the team to win 60 percent of the games that I start as pitcher."

Measurable. *An error:* "I want to be the best player on the basketball team." It's specific — there is just one outcome that is sought, but how would players know if they achieved the goal? If an award is presented for best player, the outcome is measurable; but if no award exists, then the player is going after a target that is not defined. Shooting for nebulous targets doesn't provide the incentive required to push oneself to new limits. There is no way at the end of the season for the young athlete to say, "I was a success as evidenced by achieving my objective." *The correction:* A better objective would be: "I want to average eight points, four rebounds, three steals, and 60 percent free-throw accuracy for the first half of the season."

Also, a young player may not have control over his goal of being the best player if a player as great as Ken Griffey, Jr. is on his team. Encourage your child to set goals that produce outcomes over which he has control. For example, a high school girl can set the goal of running a certain time in the half-mile which she believes will earn her first place at the state championships. The goal of running this specific and measurable time, an outcome over which she has control, is better than a goal of winning the state championship.

This example became poignantly clear in Oregon during 1991. An eighteen-year-old transfer student from Mozambique, Maria Mutola, won the state half-mile championship. She already was an Olympic athlete and ran the fastest half-mile in the world the next year! Any Oregon girl who competed against Mutola should still have the possibility of feeling like a winner by accomplishing a personal objective.

Achievable. *An error:* Young kids desperately want to be great. Wanting to be the best can lead to the faulty goal-setting practice of selecting unrealistic short-term objectives such as performing triple axles and unseating Michele Kwan as the world champion figure skater. Every child can become his or her best, but not everyone can become a world champion. Parents should remain vigilant for goals and objectives which, because they are too difficult, set the child up for failure.

The correction: Impress upon young athletes that the road to greatness is a process of small but consistent improvements. The goal of running a five-minute mile logically comes before the goal of running a four-minute mile. Running a four-minute mile in high school is achievable; three runners have done it (but none in the last twenty years). A young freshman runner may have the achievable dream of being the fourth sub-four-minute miler, and the dream could be well within his innate ability. Proper goal setting is the process that could make his dream come true. In the beginning, the ultimate goal of running a four-minute mile is not the target — there are intermediate goals and objectives that come first. SMART goals turn dreams into reality.

Relevant. *An error:* "I want to bench press two hundred pounds," is an irrelevant physical fitness objective for a teenage boy who is aspiring to become a varsity tennis player. The time spent in the weight room probably would bring him closer to a goal if it were spent on the tennis court.

The correction: The objective must be relevant to the goal and individual strengths and weaknesses. Ask young athletes why their goals and objectives are meaningful to *them,* and how the fulfillment of these will bring them something they value. "Because my big sister did it," or "Other people will think I am brave," are not relevant reasons to justify athletic goals.

It is through setting relevant goals, goals that are important to the individual, that one becomes self-responsible. As adults, we should help young people formulate their goals, but we should not hand them to them. If they are willing to own their goals, and realize that the motivation for a worthwhile goal comes from within them, then they are moving toward a more self-responsible level as a person. They are growing in character.

Timely. *An error:* "Someday I am going to have a zero handicap in golf." That date could be so far in the future for a ten-year-old, that it is not possible to set SMART objectives. Young athletes should aspire for outcomes that are near enough in terms of time that some form of action (objective) is imperative right now. Without a time target, procrastination can set in and become a habit.

The correction: A goal is not a call to action until it has a time component affiliated with it. A SMART goal, and the plan that accompanies it, spells out the day-by-day actions that must be taken in order to complete objectives on the specified date. A ten-year-old's concept of time is different from an adult's; short-term goals for young people can be very short — even two or three weeks. A timely objective might be to hit three left-handed lay-ups in a row within two weeks or to make 30 percent of three-point shots in practice.

The athletic season for youth sports programs is frequently as short as nine weeks. In order to impart the concept that goals build upon goals until the ultimate outcome is achieved, the entire goal-setting process, from formulation to completion — or failure, as is often the case — must be accelerated to fit the season.

--.--.--.--.--.--.--.--.--.--.--.--.--.--.--.-

Save the Day

Clear Your (Mental) Work Space

Using your brain as a memory bank or idea file blocks creativity and raises anxiety. Reduce your anxiety by writing down your ideas and options as you think of them. The left brain is the center for memory, logic and reasoning, observing and concentration. Creativity and feelings are functions of the right brain. A clogged left brain blocks creativity and feelings.

Clearing the left brain "working space" of memory responsibilities improves creativity. Write down memory "ticklers" about those items you need to remember. Fortified with a written memory booklet (daily planner) always in your possession, and your working space cleared, problem solving will be more creative.

Process Goals and Outcome Goals

One of our friends, Lyle Nelson, relied upon goal-setting techniques to help him make four Olympic teams. Lyle approached every season and each big race with four to six goals. "I have always been made to feel like a success," Lyle told us. "When I was young, I was complimented on my performances. When I was older, I had to find reasons to compliment myself because good performances might go unnoticed. To do this, to have the reason to praise myself, I set an abundant number of goals — always. On every occasion, I was certain to achieve some of the goals and could acknowledge that I was a success in some manner."

"My goals were of two kinds: process goals and outcome goals. The night before a big race I would write down two or three outcome goals and two or three process goals on a three-by-five card. The last thing I looked at before starting my final warm-up for the race was the goals on the card."

"Process goals," Nelson said, "are elements that I have total control over. To get to the race with plenty of time to warm-up; to stay relaxed on all the uphill climbs; to maintain positive thoughts throughout the event. These are all process goals. Such goals make sure that you go through the right events to achieve your outcome goals." Outcome goals are different: to always place in the top three; to make 50 percent of my shots; to earn a position on the varsity (Olympic) team.

Encourage your young athlete to set both process and outcome goals. In the long run, consistent application of the proper process is perhaps the most important determinant of success — in sports and in life. Outcome goals help us keep our focus on the results we want in life. They are the targets, the beacons that determine the direction of our actions.

Goals Are About More Than Winning

As adults, we make value decisions for our children. Teaching the value of competition can be particularly confusing, and somewhat complex, for both the parent and child. Our Western society bestows too much admiration — even eulogizes — sports winners. We, as authors, disagree with the famous quote, "Winning isn't everything; it is the only thing." This saying overlooks the value of character building in sports, which, in our way of thinking, is the chief objective of competition. Regardless of our opinion, however, it remains a near guarantee that your child will encounter numerous critical situations in life during which "winning" is thought to be the only acceptable outcome. Unless society changes radically, our children will be competing to win a major contract, to win a job opening, to win someone's affection. We are living in an increasingly competitive culture.

As a parent, you have to decide to what extent you are going to teach your child to compete. Sports can provide you, a parent, with excellent opportunities to impart the value, as you see it, of competing to win. The goals you and your child set highly influence the child's attitudes and values toward "competing to win."

Fear of Success

Many young athletes, at certain times, are poised to accomplish their goals, when suddenly, they sabotage themselves — either intentionally or subconsciously — and fail to perform the not-so-difficult step that would achieve the goal. A surprisingly large number of basketball players over the years have been candid enough to tell one of the authors that they were reluctant to take shots during a game because if they were successful their parents and coach would expect them to perform at these levels all the time. It was easier to deal with them by not showing much improvement, rather than for the athletes to raise their stress levels by being held to a higher level of performance.

Highly talented track runners might not put out 100 percent because they know that once a new PR (personal record) is established, the coach will only push them harder to go to the next level. Although they are gifted with the ability to do better, their reward structure says the benefits and pressures of running faster are not worth the extra effort. Perhaps these youngsters' desire is simply to run on a team with their buddies; the personal glory they might attain by pushing to the limit is irrelevant to them. It's okay for athletes to feel this way, and their feelings need to be considered before parents and coaches push to achieve new performance levels.

Another form of self-sabotage resulting from fear of success is creating excuses prior to the competition. Excuses such as partying late before a big game, picking an argument with a parent or sibling, creating a relationship crisis, all give athletes an excuse when explaining to the coach (or themselves) why they didn't perform as well as they could have. A pattern of these self-inflicted excuses is really a telegram asking for help, and parents should learn to recognize and heed these calls.

Conclusion

Parenting the gifted athlete is both fun and challenging. Talent usually gravitates to those areas where it experiences success. With their physical blessings, they will find success in sports and, in most cases, want to become more and more involved. The athlete's high sports involvement will pull the entire family in that direction. Be sensitive to the exceptional athlete in your family, if you have one. He or she may have the stuff of champions in him or her, but it will be up to you to encourage the spark of greatness until it is strong enough to flame and make its own bold light.

10

Turning Setbacks Into Comebacks

Success is progress along a pathway toward a goal. Because life has to be lived forward, not in the past, the pathway to success is not clearly marked; at times we are pioneers. When we stray too far from the most direct route, we are fortunate to receive a message that we're off the preferred path. These messages are confirmation of error, or temporary setbacks, but in the long run they are the guidance system that takes us to the goal.

To eliminate setbacks would be to eliminate the adventuresome attitude of traveling an uncharted course. Life fully lived is about venturing forth, taking risks, and leading, rather than following, the conformist's path. This important chapter informs parents and young athletes how to take corrective action to get on the best course.

It is certain that your young athlete is going to experience setbacks — temporary failures, if you will — in sports, and you wouldn't want it to be any other way. It's going to hurt a little, both for you and the player, to live through a setback, especially one that follows the player's best effort. But within these trying moments are character-building lessons that prepare youngsters for the trials and tribulations of life.

Knowing how to turn setbacks into comebacks is a common characteristic of successful people from all walks of life. One of the world's most enduring coaches, Confucius, said it best: "Our greatest glory is not in never failing, but in rising every time we fail."

The formula for success is also known as the school of hard knocks: it involves trying, failing and getting back up, one step closer to a personal victory.

Much ado and dramatization is made by the media of the setbacks famous athletes have endured while competing under the national spotlight. TV spectators during the 1984 Olympics had dozens of chances to see world record holder Mary Decker Slaney fall during the 5000-meter run. Her comeback took twelve years to materialize when she qualified for the 1996 Olympic team. It's easy to believe that setbacks are isolated to those who are going for the gold. This is not so. The majority of young athletes has chosen to compete in recreational programs, and at times they will not achieve the personal outcomes that are important to them.

Regardless of one's chosen level of competition, the following information can help turn a setback into a comeback. Mary Slaney bounced back to make another Olympic team, and your child can bounce from occasional setbacks that are unavoidable in sports.

Save the Day

Score the Day's Wins and Losses
Even on your worst days, odds are you will have more wins than losses. Place objectives you achieved in the win column; only those attempts that received final denial are losses. Everything else is still undecided.

During the day keep a running score of your wins and losses. Call or visit your positive partner and tell him or her about your favorite win. Beat yesterday! "I had a 26-3 day today!"

Analyzing Setbacks is Essential for Success

Experiencing a setback is not a travesty: not learning from it is. Typical setbacks for young athletes include not getting a chance to play, losing an important game, not personally scoring any points during the game, running (swimming, biking) slower than anticipated, or injuring oneself prior to an important event. As soon as the emotional or physical sting of the setback has abated, it's time to make a practical analysis of why the setback occurred.

Many prescriptions are available for comebacks after physical setbacks. However, especially for young athletes, emotional setbacks may go untreated even though they have greater impact on a person's future if not immediately remediated. Young athletes need help from their coach or parents in staging a comeback.

Analyzing the root cause of the setback is undertaken in a positive tone of finding a solution to a temporary

problem. By focusing on the solution, and not the defi-
ciency, the child's self-confidence and determination can be
quickly returned. Unfortunately, some sports teams do not
want to deal with "bad news." Their main thrust is
rewarding heroes and reliving the positive, heroic moments
in the game. By ignoring setbacks, those who most need
help to achieve future successes don't get the information
they need to improve. Many times the setback occurred for
reasons beyond their control, and yet they perceive themselves to be weak or inferior when in fact they did their part
well.

Athletes (and parents and coaches too) should learn
that reviewing a performance is just as important as
planning it or executing it. Sitting down and discussing the
outcome, whether it was good or poor, should be so routine
that it causes little, if any, added stress. Parents who make a
priority of discussing setbacks (the biggest skill is
listening), report that these are among the most valuable
moments in child-rearing. When reviewing setbacks with
your child, make sure the player realizes that analyzing the
setback is not a procedure of placing blame or an occasion
for chastisement.

If setbacks are identified and dealt with properly,
young athletes who are committed to sports should emerge
from the experience with more motivation and knowledge
to continue. If a setback continually reappears and is
accompanied by little concern from the athlete, then
perhaps parents and player should review the core values
and beliefs underlining their sports participation to
determine if there is a basic conflict.

The Root Causes of Setbacks

"The grass was too slippery."

"I felt tired today."

"I was too worried about my math final."

"I went out too fast and burned out."

"I get nervous when you come and watch the games."

"I don't know, maybe I'm just not good enough."

The foregoing are all valid statements that probably reflect some of the reasons for the setback, but they are not the root cause of the problem. Being tired, for example, is a symptom of being overextended, or physically overtrained, or perhaps mentally exhausted. Discovering the root cause is the entry point for determining the best way to make a comeback.

The real conditions for a setback can be classified into the following six categories. Parents, coaches and players should judge the root causes of setbacks to be neither negative or positive. They are the existing conditions; accept them and determine a new course of action.

1. Inadequate preparation
2. Inadequate ability (physical or mental)
3. The goal was unrealistically difficult
4. Careless performance
5. Bad luck
6. The system failed the athlete

1. Inadequate preparation. Being ill-prepared is not necessarily an indication of poor motivation. Family considerations, academic priorities, injuries, or the need to work after school, are all valid reasons for being less prepared than the competition — those who might focus solely on sports. To be beaten by someone who is better prepared doesn't mean the "loser" has failed. This is a difficult concept for young players to grasp; parents need to be there to help explain this and to remind the competitive athlete that the ultimate goal is to win in life, not sports, and that in your eyes he or she is a winner, no matter what the scoreboard says.

On the other hand, if peers are practicing more, and your player is on a team that has a high desire to win, or if the goal requires a serious commitment, then lack of preparation has a different connotation. It must be impressed upon the athlete that the will to prepare must be commensurate with the challenge. World champion David Kimes said, "The will to prepare is more important than the will to win." Wanting to win does not give you a competitive advantage — everyone wants to win. The difference is in preparing yourself to win, both physically and mentally.

Today's youth live in a "want-it-now" generation where overnight successes are glamorized and portrayed by the media as something available to all of us. Young people are seldom aware of the enormous amount of work and preparation that was done to be an "overnight success." Sports teach the most reliable way to be successful: work diligently and follow a step-by-step plan toward the goal.

The comeback. First, determine how much effort (time, money, energy) it will take for your child to have a reasonable chance of accomplishing outcomes desired from sports. Then ask if the potential outcomes are compatible with other commitments and choices. Sit down together and make a tentative weekly schedule and confirm that there is time to meet the sports demand as well as other essential, or preferred, time demands. We have discovered that lack of time is seldom the limiting factor; instead, the limiting factor lies in the player's choice to spend time doing other things or, in other words, prioritizing. These "other things" may in fact be more important and beneficial to the child; identifying this can reduce any guilt associated with not feeling successful.

More competitive athletes need to recognize that it is their responsibility to allocate the necessary time if they want to have a chance to earn the rewards available through sports. A lack of motivation to prepare always indicates that the rewards associated with other choices are seen as more readily available or attractive. That's why it is so important for parents and coaches to point out the progress young athletes are making. This acknowledgment is one of the most cherished rewards for youth. The reason that "success begets success" is that the initial success felt good, and the ensuing successes are a continued pursuit of the same good feelings.

Finally, it is important to look at preparation over an extended period of time. Beginners in a sport — and everyone starts as a beginner — can't be expected to look cool or make great plays. The fear of "I don't want to look foolish" is endemic in youth sports. This is especially true for adolescents who did not learn athletic skills at early ages. Youngsters have a tendency to blow early mistakes out of proportion and deduce, "I'm just not any good at athletics," when the more accurate appraisal is that they haven't yet gained the skills. Impress upon your athlete that it is okay to be a beginner .

2. Inadequate ability. At times in sport — and life — youngsters have to accept the fact that they were bettered by the competition. The competition's advantage might have been physical, mental, or both; it could be a fortunate inheritance (size and strength) or the product of focus, and hard work (skill and attitude). It doesn't matter how the competition achieved their advantage; they have it, and determination alone will not consistently enable a lesser-talented player to compete on a par.

A future Olympian worked very hard his junior year in high school to be a starting player on the football team. Not being very fast, his only chance was to be an offensive lineman. To stack the odds even higher against him, he weighed only 165 pounds. When his team played the Parma Panthers, the opposing lineman was Don Trent, a chiseled 200-plus-pounder who also won the heavyweight state wrestling championships. Despite the future Olympian's best efforts, he couldn't keep Trent from crashing through the line and making tackle after tackle. Years later, Trent still remembered the game and said, "You know, I still remember the game I played against your brother; he gave 110 percent of himself but just didn't have the size or strength to keep me from running right over him."

The comeback. When your child is hopelessly outclassed (leagues are organized to try and prevent mismatches, but they still happen) and has made his best effort, then the athlete and parents must deal with the cause of the mismatch of ability. Dealing with the cause is proactive; allowing the child to feel inadequate is passive. There are two active choices: help your child to improve in ability, or match the levels of ability better. Ability improves when children are moderately challenged, but not when they are overwhelmed. There are times when young athletes should say to themselves, "I may not win, but everybody is going to respect my effort when it's over." We know a coach who told his athletes, "If you can't win, make the one ahead of you break the record."

Encouraging a child to play her best, and at the same time inferring that she may not be state championship material, takes quality parent/athlete interaction. False encouragement and unrealistic hopes set a young athlete up for a big fall.

Constantly reassure your child that the best he can do is good enough. Match the child with competition or challenges that equal his ability. Within the family treat all levels of athletic participation as equally important. One thing we have learned as coaches is that the "big time" is where the child is currently playing. The immediate thrill of hitting a home run is equal whether the batter plays on a recreation team, select team or school team. This is all that young athletes can be expected to do — to make an earnest attempt to reach their goals. Young athletes feel like heroes when they play well against players of their own ability.

Remind them that individuals develop at their own rate. Numerous professional athletes were also-rans in their earlier years.

3. The goal was unrealistically difficult. As noted in the previous chapter, parents and coaches help young athletes set inspiring and challenging goals — goals that may be out of current reach, but not out of sight. Sometimes the difficulty of the goal is underestimated and, once striving for it, parents, athletes and coaches realize that it was much more difficult than originally anticipated. Young athletes don't always accurately perceive the difficulty of the goal — after all, others have made it — and interpret the failure as a personal shortcoming. They need to realize that they accomplished a lot by making an earnest attempt to reach their goal. When the overall goal is defined by a set of objectives, the feeling of failure can be avoided, even if the goal isn't reached, when measurable progress toward the individual objectives has taken place.

The comeback. As adults, we know that failing to reach a difficult goal, especially in the first attempt, does not make a young player a failure — but he might not know this. Remind him that Edison didn't invent the light bulb on his first try. Very few things of significance are achieved in the first attempt. Ernest Hemingway wrote the final chapter to *A Farewell to Arms* thirty-eight times! When asked why he labored so diligently, he answered, "To get it right!"

If the goal is truly out of sight, now and perhaps permanently, replace the goal with a realistic challenge and go after the new one with the same gusto. If the original goal is still a possibility, suggest to the player that he focus on the interim objectives and use these objectives as stepping stones to the original goal. One solution may be to readjust the time span and try again.

4. Careless performance. Most youngsters haven't learned the mental skill of concentration. In very young athletes this skill is rare; in older ones it's often underdeveloped. That is one of the reasons they have inconsistent performances. For parents it is frustrating to watch their child play a great game one week and then exhibit an error-riddled performance the following week. But this uneven performance demonstrates the natural development curve for children. They should not be scolded for this, no more than they should be reprimanded for failing to master a new concept in math.

Careless performances can result from being overconfident, from having a preoccupied mind, or from focusing on the wrong element of the game. A baseball pitcher shouldn't be concentrating only on the runner on second while trying to strike out the batter. The pitcher's focus must encompass both the batter and the runner.

━ ━·━·━·━·━·━·━·━·━·━·━·━·━·━·━·━

The comeback. To combat carelessness, coaches and parents need to interrupt the random thoughts of the player and give a cue that invokes the right focus. For example, a coach might say to a shortstop, "As soon as the batter steps into the batter's box, I want you to think about where to throw the ball if she hits it to you. Don't worry about anything else; I know you can do it." Another strategy is to practice a specific skill (or rehearse a particular athletic situation) so many times that the performance becomes automatic — a subconscious action. Then players can think about something else and simultaneously make the correct play. Astronauts can spend upwards of ten years working on their space mission. They do it only once but have done it in their minds hundreds of times.

Skill performance and mental focus errors can be reduced, but not totally eliminated by practice and attentiveness. Visualization (a training tool which is also called mental imagery) is an excellent tool for reducing careless errors. Youth need uninterrupted time and a place to imagine performing at their best or rehearsing a particular skill. Parents, by simply asking older players to explain strategies and responsibilities can enhance focus and reduce careless errors.

5. Bad luck. Luck plays a part in sports. Bad luck alone is seldom the culprit for a setback, but young athletes shouldn't feel low — or accountable — for those situations in which bad luck played a significant role. (Bad luck is beyond anyone's control, and among the best advice a young athlete will ever hear is: Don't concern yourself with things you cannot control.) Equipment breaks, referees make mistakes, as do coaches, and balls take a bad bounce on uneven fields. There is a degree of uncertainty in sports;

it's part of the fun and excitement. The best don't always win; it's the same in life.

The comeback. It's okay for a parent to end a pep talk about setbacks with the statement, "I think it was mostly bad luck; let's get back out there and try again." However, if parents repeatedly use the bad-luck rationalization, they are probably overlooking the root cause and not providing their young player, who wants to improve, the needed feedback to do so. If adults provide excuses for their young athlete, the athlete may miss the learning point and look at negative outcomes as bad luck, which is not always the case. We especially like the quote: "The harder I work, the luckier I get."

6. The system fails the athlete. To us, this is the worst type of all the setbacks, and the type this book is devoted to eliminating. Kids do not have the capability to change the system, and they are the ones rejected by it when it fails. This is why a partnership among coaches, players and parents is so crucial. When one partner suffers unreasonably, everyone is responsible for mending the system. Often the solution requires more resources than just these partners; it takes a community of business and civic support.

System failures include: 1) families that won't — or can't — support the child's sports interest; 2) schools that don't provide opportunities for those who can't make the starting team; 3) insufficient athletic activities within the community, and 4) mistakes by unqualified or uncaring coaches.

The comeback. Single parents have a particularly tough chore in supporting their children's sports interest. There's just not enough time in the day. Grandparents, uncles and older siblings can be great surrogates. In today's society, the extended family has a new orientation; it may include neighbors who would like to be involved with youngsters. There may be a retired senior who wants to get off the porch and into the cheering section for her favorite neighborhood boy or girl.

The competition for time in the school gym is fierce. Schools can't provide coaching for everyone. Is there a local business that can help? The tiny town of McCall, Idaho, proudly calls itself "Ski Town U.S.A." For years the local lumber mill sent a bus and an employee (who was an expert skier) to the grade school to pick up the young skiers and take them to the ski hill. The driver was also the coach. The fact that McCall placed Olympic skiers in every winter Olympics but two between 1952 and 1988 shows the success of such volunteer efforts. The mill owners well knew the value of youth sports to a community.

Facilities don't have to be perfect or expensive. One determined individual who can lobby the city leaders can turn a vacant field or parking lot into an athletic facility. Kids need adults to create opportunities. Being all dressed up and having nowhere to go is a most demoralizing situation. It breeds hopelessness and delinquency. Adults who want to make a significant contribution to youth should explore creative ways to involve them in sports.

Parents, if the right team isn't available for your child, considering organizing a team, or a league. You can find out how to order uniforms (if you even need them), reserve facilities, buy equipment or anything else needed to get started. You can start a program with a "no-cuts" policy or one that doesn't even keep score. Concerned parents started the Special Olympics, which now services tens of thousands of mentally challenged athletes.

All of the previous examples are sports-specific types of setbacks which, if handled correctly, can turn out to be valuable long-term lessons in life.

Not Being Selected for a Team

It happens thousands of times every year: young boys or girls who desperately want to play on a school or all-star team (band, school play) go through the tryout procedure, perform up to their ability, and are told that they aren't good enough to make the team. Not only do they lose their vision of scoring the winning goal, they lose the time that would have been spent with their friends on the team.

It's difficult to prepare children for this disappointing experience. Compounding the emotional hurt is the message parents commonly tell their children: "If you try hard enough, long enough, you will eventually succeed." But they did try hard, and they didn't succeed. Parents can sympathize with the letdown the children feel if they, themselves, have ever missed a highly coveted promotion or sought-after contract in business.

The family should immediately come to the rescue of the deflated athlete. A little "we love you" talk is the first intervention. Then comes Plan B. Is there another sports program? What do we have to do to improve for the next tryouts? Can the family fill the void with family sports outings? Many kids started kayaking, rock climbing or weight lifting as a means of replacing the agony of not being on the team. They become experts in their new endeavor and learn lessons and skills as valuable as if they had made the team. A concerted family effort will help the athlete rebound from being cut. (Families can also take an active role in working with schools to offer sports programs for other than star-quality performers.)

When a youth thinks he was unfairly cut, it's very difficult for parents, who usually aren't able to watch the selection procedure or know the coach's mind, to take a stance defending the child's ability, the system, or the coach. The one thing parents can support is the child — as a person. Being sympathetic to the child's feelings is different than passing judgment on the situation which provoked the feelings. However, parents should be completely comfortable asking the coach why their child was cut; with this information the family can prepare for the next tryouts. Schools and select teams sometimes have prescribed regulations for handling tryouts. You'll want to know what they are before tryouts begin.

The disappointment of being cut can be reduced if the athlete receives advance mental preparation for the tryouts from the coach and parents. The following two letters are used by author John Devine to prepare young players and their parents for the tryout procedure for the all-star basketball teams he coaches. The letters differ from how a school coach would prepare interscholastic athletes for the team selection process. However, it's important that *all* coaches have a way of making athletes feel worthy for having attended tryouts.

Letter One: To parents and players participating in tryouts for select/all-star team:

I am glad that you have decided to attend our _____ team tryout. I admire all the players who have placed themselves in a risky situation; it takes a lot of courage to put yourself on the line and compete against other talented athletes. We will be selecting at least _____ and no more than _____ players; there will be more than that number at tryouts. If you are not selected, you will be selling yourself short if you look at this as failing. You have already done what most adults never do: you have taken a risk in front of peers and family with no assurance of the outcome. You have left your comfort zone and are to be congratulated for doing so. That is reward in itself!

For those of you selected, you need to be aware that some not chosen may have had a bad day or that too many fine athletes were trying out for the same position, and we could only take a certain number of them. It would be a mistake to look at those not selected as being losers; in some ways they may learn more about themselves and the true value of sport than those selected will. It takes a special person to accept and learn and grow from not getting what they want.

Before deciding to accept an invitation to try out, you need to be aware of some things. Since we view this team as a place to continue to work on individual and team skills, we will be having regularly scheduled practices. Last year we had _____ per week, and the players and parents seemed to work that into their schedules. We plan to practice _____ weeks this year. Because this is a team game, the players should understand that they are expected to be at practices and games. We'll play in a number of tournaments, so you should be prepared to play on Saturdays and maybe an occasional Sunday. In unusual circumstances we can make an occasional exception; however, if you are playing on other teams or have other obligations which will create conflicts, then _____ will not be the best team for your sports activities. I am NOT an advocate of playing only one sport or giving up other important activities and strongly encourage those who want a broader athletic background to play more than one sport. _____ will be for those who have made a personal decision to pursue it because [name of sport] satisfies all their athletic needs. You need to make a decision before we select a team. If you prefer to play in a different setting, please let me know, and I can give you some alternatives.

Everyone needs to know that my style of coaching is more centered on team play rather than developing one or two superstars. I do not emphasize points scored...actually, I rarely look at a scorebook! I am more interested in effort, unselfish team play, positive attitude, responsiveness, hustle, determination, etc. These abilities carry over for a lifetime and are more valuable than points. We will NOT play to win at all costs! We also will NOT have equal playing time. Success will come from working and learning from each other. If my approach is compatible with yours, I am positive we'll have a great time!

Letter Two: Given to players on the final day of tryouts:
Dear Athlete,

Thank you for coming to the last tryout today. I know you all have taken a risk, and I think you have shown a great deal of courage by putting your skills on display. I have asked a number of people to assist me in making team selections, and I will pay a great deal of attention to their evaluations. I know you all will be given a fair chance to be chosen.

I will call each of you tonight and let you know the results of tryouts. You should be aware that many famous players were not selected for teams they wanted to play for (Michael Jordan was cut once as a teenager!) yet learned a lot of positive things from the experience. You'll want to re-read my letter regarding tryouts which I gave you before the selection process began. It tells you how much I value your risk taking and how proud I am that you came tonight!

Winston Churchill on Commitment

Perhaps no twentieth-century person has displayed a more indomitable will, a more positive attitude than Winston Churchill, who led England from the emotional lows of World War II to the satisfaction of victory. One of Churchill's speeches, slightly adapted for this book, reads:

No matter what happens, we just don't quit.... If you have a goal, work hard to get there. The only way you will fail to eventually reach your goal is if you quit. If you aren't in condition, it will be easier to quit. If you haven't sacrificed, it will be a lot easier to quit, because you will have little to lose. All quitters are good losers. When you quit once, it's easier to quit a second time, and then it becomes a habit. One of the most important qualities an athlete must have is a strong mental attitude. Some call it heart, the refusal to ever give up. There will be times when you lose. If you must lose, lose with pride. Go down swinging. Then get up and practice harder; push yourself so next time you will be more prepared to win. The great person never, never, never quits.

Risk of Injury in Youth Sports

It would be improper to close this chapter without including material on the risk of injuries in sports, since they certainly affect goal-setting and career objectives for young athletes, whether they are gifted, extraordinary, or just wholesome and average.

Sports injury statistics are rarely compared with non-athletic high-risk activities. The fact is sports injuries are not high-risk factors to amateur players. Youngsters are safer from serious injury, statistically, on the football field than riding a bicycle. They are safer from catastrophic injury while wrestling than when riding in a car. More injuries, per participant hour, occur at home than in gymnasiums. When coaches have been given proper risk-reduction instruction (most schools make this training mandatory) the incidence of injury is further reduced. Great care should be taken to question community-based teams and to evaluate the coach's knowledge of risk prevention. Statistically, the safest environment for your child, during after-school hours, is while participating in a properly supervised and certified community or school activity.

Research shows that athletes under stress, while participating in sports, are more prone to injury. Risk control includes stress reduction, playing by the rules, good coaching of safe skills, sportsmanship, plenty of rest, good conditioning, and *never, never, never* allowing a return-to-play decision to be based on the importance of the game rather than the importance of the player.

Total rehabilitation of an injury is risk control. Reinjuries are the most serious, hardest to remediate, and most likely to occur when the original injury is not completely healed. A comparison to professional heroes who "play hurt" and claim "no pain, no gain" is inappropriate risk management strategy for young athletes.

Athletic association rules, parents should understand, are enforced in part for the safety of players, to determine if they have permission and are physically fit to participate.

Parents should also be very much aware that the sports violence observable on television is not an acceptable part of the risk of participating in youth athletics. Pro athletes have publicly announced intentions to harm opponents, usually "within the rules." Prior to 1970, courts ruled that risks were inherent to sports. In 1962, a court ruled that "the participants in an athletic event are held to have assumed the risk of injury normally associated with the sport... voluntary participants must accept risks to which their roles expose them." However, attitudes have changed; intentional misconduct and rule-prohibited behavior are no longer considered an inherent risk of sport. In order to assume the risk, courts have usually required that the knowledge of risk be understood and the risk be voluntarily accepted. Kids, especially inexperienced youth, must understand the risks involved before they can voluntarily accept them. It is argued that *parents assume risk* by signature on "permission to play" forms. The signature also verifies having read, and thus having been warned of, the "inherent dangers" listed on the form.

Parents, as well as coaches, are responsible that players are aware of their responsibilities for personal safety and duty of care toward other players. Safety in play, playing by the rules, and proper equipment and use must all be taught and learned. Given such duties, it is legally the coach, and morally the parent, who must be confident any injury was not caused by failure to instruct. As in all other cases when the physical or emotional wellness of a young person is involved, parents need to be aware of policy *before* the incident occurs.

Parents, and coaches, have been confused from time to time about "unavoidable accidents." An unavoidable accident in sports has been defined as "not intended and which, under all the circumstances, could not have been foreseen or prevented by the exercise of reasonable precaution." Application of this definition implies liability could be that of parents or coaches, or the children they "teach". if an injury resulted from 1) behaviors intended to harm; 2) negligence in preventing situations that could or should have been foreseen; or 3) failure to take reasonable precautions.

The following example should give parents and coaches a clear definition of "preventable behavior:"

A football tackling dummy hanging from the goalpost of the practice field displayed the jersey and number of the leading scorer on a high school team. Players from the opposing team were instructed to "blast" the dummy on their way to practice and again as practice ended, while teammates and coaches watched and cheered.

Was behavior being taught with intent to harm? Could injury be foreseen? Were reasonable precautions made?

The school district insurance company agreed the broken leg suffered by the leading scorer in the first quarter was an *avoidable accident.* Medical and rehabilitation costs were voluntarily paid by the insurance company. The coach and entire team visited the injured player and apologized.

Considering the legal duties and responsibilities of coaching, parents should support the safety decisions and actions of coaches and other leaders of youth activities. Here are some sound ideas to enhance safety in sport:

- Coaches must teach rules of sport and codes of conduct.
- Coaches and parents cannot condone conduct that violates the rules.
- Coaches and players may be liable for unsportsman-like conduct or recklessness.
- The school or institution has a duty to exercise due care in hiring and supervision of coaching personnel.
- Coaches (and organizations) have responsibility and legal duties to:
    - properly instruct (rules, behavior, conditioning, progression).
    - warn of inherent dangers.
    - provide proper supervision (program, transportation, personnel).
    - provide health care (equipment, injuries, warm-ups, emergency).
    - enforce rules and regulations (sport rules, eligibility, state).
    - classify and group participants (skill, age, gender, maturity, size).
    - provide constitutional rights.
    - provide safe transportation (driver, vehicle inspection, insurance).
    - employ/assign qualified personnel (volunteers, job descriptions).

— protect spectators/patrons (officials, crowd control, facilities).

The High Risk Sports:
A Surprise

Parents should be aware of a thirteen-year study (1979-1992) of 60,000 high school athletes representing twenty urban schools which resulted in some surprising myth-breakers. Conducted by Dr. Steven G. Rice, Director of the Athletic Health Care System of the University of Washington, the study disclosed that "The number one sport for injury was girls' cross country...far ahead in total injuries, first in significant injuries and tied for second in major injuries."

Dr. Rice found that only three of the top seven "high-risk sports" matched their reputation for injuries: football (second), wrestling (third), and girls' gymnastics (sixth) in number of injuries per 100 athletes. The other four might surprise parents: girls' cross country (first), boys' cross country (fifth), and girls' and boys' soccer (fourth and seventh).

Following the top seven sports identified as "high-injury sports" by Dr. Rice, a second grouping consisted of girls' basketball, boys' basketball, volleyball, softball, baseball and boys' track. Three "low-risk" sports, often co-ed coached, were swimming, tennis and golf. Dr. Rice also concluded fall sports have a higher incidence of injury than spring sports, and girls' sports had higher rates of injury than identical boys' sports.

Team Family Risk Control

There are no youth athletic activities without risk of injury. There are high risk and low risk, but none are zero risk. The importance and severity of most injuries to players is measured in loss of playing time. Injury rate statistics hold little comfort for the parents of an injured youth. Statistics should, however, convince parents, players, and coaches that any and all safety instruction, discipline, learning actions are to be appreciated and encouraged. Adequate insurance needs to be purchased by parents whose boys or girls are playing sports. You'll need to talk to your insurance agent and school administrator to be certain you're covered.

11

It Isn't Just Sports We're Talking About

Victory Beyond the Scoreboard has addressed much more than participating in sports and other after-school activities; it has advocated an approach to success that youth and adults alike can use to build confidence, competence and self-satisfaction. It is this approach, this way of life, which far outdistances the significance of sports. In that sense, this is not just a sports book.

While the authors would like your child to experience success in sports and other activities, their ultimate desire is for your child to achieve success in life. Even though our analogies are often extracted from sports situations, the message is just as pertinent for those who choose other activities during their free time. Sports does not have an exclusive claim for developing well-adjusted, productive and happy people.

Success is not measured only by how far a football can be thrown or how quickly someone can run. Success is meeting psychological, social, and physical challenges with a positive attitude and learned skills. All organized youth activities can help America's youth meet these challenges — the challenges of life.

The Most Important Choice is to Choose

The decision to be proactive in choosing an activity is as important as the choice itself. It has been demonstrated over and over that there is a strong correlation between personal success and participation in activities outside the home. Parents wield a huge influence (sometimes even while trying to remain passive) and, if properly informed, can guide their children to the best activities for them. Whether singing in the choir or hitting home runs, there is a lot more to participating than mastering skills; teamwork, family responsibility, sportsmanship, positive attitudes, and how to have fun are equally important lessons. Participation in any competitive activity which is administered correctly serves a valuable purpose — the transformation of eager children into happy and responsible adults.

When Schools Curtail Activities

To get a better picture of the positive impact activities have on *schools*, it's worth repeating the question: What happens when activities are curtailed or eliminated? Schools experience:

1. An increase in outgoing transfers by student leaders and activity participants to schools with ample programs.
2. Formation of active parent and community groups to retain activities.
3. Increases in number of dropouts; law enforcement

incidents, including gang-related activities; and school disciplinary problems (primarily conduct code violations), which all correlate directly to the percentage of program cuts.
4. Lowering of the school's academic achievement (GPA averages).

When Schools Retain Activities

The positive impact on *individuals* who participate in activities is too valuable to be denied. The State of Washington discovered that students who are involved in after-school activities will have:
1. GPA averages .7 higher than the overall school GPA.
2. Seven fewer absences per year than the overall school average.
3. Higher GPA during season of participation than when they are not performing.
4. Fewer than 15 percent of the overall school disciplinary problems.
5. Higher rates of completed homework turned in on time.
6. Less truancy and fewer classes missed.
7. Higher graduation rates (over 96 percent graduate).
8. Higher advanced education and employment rates.

Turn Your Concern Into Action

With benefits like these, concerned parents, communities, school boards, and elected officials need to unite in support of the tremendous advantages sports and other activities provide in developing our future leaders. School boards, even in the face of budget cuts and time constraints, must continue providing these programs.

Coaches, players and family, when banded together, possess an enormous capability to ensure that everyone involved in youth activities adhere to the highest standards of behavior. By combining resources with others of the same value-based ideals, this united front can collectively prevent forms of physical and mental abuse.

If sports is to continue as a viable training ground for leaders of tomorrow, all partners must express their views and strive for constant program improvements. Apathy and miscommunication have done more to restrict the growth of youth activities than financial limitations.

Parents are committed to wanting the best for their children. They are unyielding in their belief that the ultimate outcome is "to become the best one can be"...the best Connor, the best Kelsey, the best Nathan, the best McKenzie. Youth activities must make *all* participants feel like winners. Only a few will be rewarded by reaching competitive excellence; the system must also benefit and reward the greater majority

By focusing on the desired outcomes and taking appropriate action to correct counterproductive behaviors, parents can — one game at a time — play an indispensable role. The game plan presented in *Victory Beyond the Scoreboard* best prepares parents to address these issues. Parents who lack understanding of the real value, philosophy, and operating norms of youth sports have not been effective agents of change — often due to their confrontational approach. Unfortunately, this approach can put coaches and/or administrators in a defensive or avoidance mode, which inhibits the benefits of a healthy partnership.

With new insights parents will now feel empowered to deal with situations harmful to players and families.

Consider the following poem written by a longtime coach, teacher, administrator, and lifelong advocate of youth sports.

Do It Today

Do you ever think at dawn or night
of letters kind you meant to write —
But didn't.

Do you ever think at the close of day
of kindly words you meant to say —
But didn't.

Do you ever think as one day folds into another
that tomorrow I will —
But didn't.

And then —
Promise yourself before this day is done
you will accomplish just one — *just one.*

And then —
Promise yourself before many days have passed
you will accomplish many *beautiful tasks.*

And then —
As you approach the day that your sun might set
you can look at what you haven't accomplished yet.

And then —
Those around you might say
what will we do without those sunny rays...

You know, I think that I wanted to accomplish all
those nice things, but I just ran out of days....

So ... why not do it today?
by George Carberry Jr.

Support the Best, Challenge the Rest

Parents need to be supportive of coaches who are doing the right thing. With little support on one hand, too much constraint on the other, and little or no compensation, coaches face formidable challenges. Despite the odds, coaches are frequently remembered by players (or other activity participants) as the one person outside their family with the greatest effect on their lives. Many coaches have gained local and nationwide acclaim for adhering to principles which may have jeopardized a short-term victory on the scoreboard and, in the process, became momentarily unpopular with other stakeholders. Countless others, in unpublicized incidents, consistently put values above winning. Parents fortunate enough to be involved with such positive role models need to encourage and thank these people. Too many ethical and value-based coaches only hear good things when teams are winning; far too few are commended following a losing season. It's not surprising that many of them feel pressured to win.

Exploring for Success

The spirit of after-school activities should be: "I can't *make* you have fun, but I can *allow* you to have fun." Perhaps Abraham Lincoln said it best: "People are about as happy as they make up their minds to be." This is the message activity directors need to emphasize because, without elements of fun, participation begins to show marked decline.

People support that which they create, understand, have confidence in, and believe to be an improvement over the present situation. To discover what they enjoy doing, young people must explore a wide variety of options. As with any exploration, there is associated risk because sometimes youth don't discover what they were looking for and get burned in the search. After-school activities fit the explorer model, and parents can curtail the randomness of the search by employing the Team Family concepts presented in Chapter Three.

As active participants in the sports scene for many decades, the authors feel strongly that sports, properly administered, play a unique role in developing the whole person. Although most young athletes experience years of fun and learn valuable life lessons, others encounter physical, moral, and mental abuse when sports programs are left unchecked or operate without accountability. Winning at all costs leaves little room for developing characteristics which add to a person's well-being. All too often these approaches grind up those who make mistakes and spit them out before they can learn lessons society so desperately wants its youth to learn.

On the other hand, sports can be a near-magical activity for bringing families closer together. It's an astonishing, albeit sad, statistic that average parents talk to their teenager for less than two minutes per day! If sports becomes the catalyst for changing this statistic, that is success in itself. In addition, if goals are achieved, and the sports experience meshes with Team Family goals, then all the partners win twice!

One Person Can Make a Difference

The vast majority of parents are good, moral, dedicated and supportive. Unfortunately, there are some parents, coaches, and fans who consistently display negative behavior with the justification that, "Whatever actions I take for the benefit of my child are okay." For too long the silent majority has condoned this behavior. If no attempt is made to correct minor indiscretions, the door is open wide for additional abuses. Negative factors, left unchecked, serve as terrible examples for easily influenced young athletes.

The following anecdote is not unique because there are many parents who are actively involved in becoming agents of change. It's noteworthy because it shows how one person can have a dramatic effect on all partners by assuming the role of making them all feel better about themselves. Not all parents have the time or natural ability to take a public role, yet they are extremely effective in their own way. Parents need not wait until they can play a major and visible role; just doing a small part can have a cumulative, monumental effect.

Bev had as much to do with the success of one of the author's teams as any drill, player, or the coach himself. This did not happen by accident; she intentionally sat with someone different at each game and shared her optimistic and positive attitude. (The most successful coaches stress the value of spending some time with each player at every practice.) She used her ability to bring out the best in people and galvanized an extremely positive support group for the players. She found time to congratulate players and parents of opposing teams and referees. She supported other parents in playing equally important though less visible roles such as parent representative, scorekeeper, and administrator. These extra duties did not prevent them from being excited fans or from offering "advice" to the coach, but it was always done in a respectful way and within the boundaries of the Partnership. This was a fun team to be around!

A life-changing event? Not really, but it is significant because it shows how a parent with some knowledge of an activity and prepared with a game plan can be an effective coach's assistant. With regard to Bev's team, do you think it really matters whether or not all games are won? If players and parents are made to feel a part of something fun and positive, they will support it. Everybody wins. Wouldn't you want your son or daughter to be on a team like this one? As more parents learn the skills of leading Team Family and participate in a true Partnership with coaches and players, there will be more teams like Bev's.

Save the Day

Take a Short Course; Learn a New Approach

Learn a new approach or how to do something new. Keep an updated list of little wish-I-knew-how-to activities you've never had time to learn. Transfer the wish list to your calendar or computer. The list should include how-to's such as "cut shopping costs," "add color to transparencies," "understand an insurance policy," "program my voice mail," "end a conversation," "deal with teenage moods," "create client memory joggers," "repair an electric cord," "learn baseball terms."

It takes personal sacrifice to achieve almost anything worthwhile. To save your day, you may need to sacrifice ego and ask for help.

Building Winners in Life

Regardless of the activity, participants can be considered winners if they are provided an opportunity to develop the following:

Acquire Personal Values. By meeting the standards of a program or coach, young people are living up to a set of values. Learning comes from "trying them on" for the duration of the activity and then adopting the best. They will realize, if the coach and program are well grounded, that values are not situational; i.e., they cannot be discarded for personal gain or convenience.

Visualize Success. To feel compelled to succeed, it is imperative to have personal goals and be willing to work for them. Having an opportunity to achieve goals draws people to activities. This is what sports should be all about. It's not just about sinking a game-winning basket or grinding out laps in the swimming pool. Seeing oneself as a winner — visualizing success — is the long-lasting benefit.

Communicate Effectively. Communication skills are so essential in families, relationships and work teams. Are young men and women successful because they can play a trombone or throw strikes? Obviously, no. To be a member of a team, to work together, communication is essential. Perhaps, for more than any other reason, youth who participate in group activities excel because they learn communication skills. Communication is more than written or spoken words. For example, finishing last in a race — but finishing with dignity — can express more about character than wearing a medal.

Acquire Needed Life Skills. Youth activities teach that skills precede success. Too many young people want instant success and recognition, and because the media usually shows only the victorious moments and not the work behind the scenes, they believe these are easily acquired or are a birthright. Youth are ill-served if they are led to believe that it takes little effort to acquire skills of math, interrelationships, art, or sports. Youth activities are educational laboratories where opportunities to develop lifelong skills are practiced and perfected.

Face the Challenge. Preparation is essential, but at some point young people must face the challenge of performing. Activities geared toward today's youth give them a chance to take center stage — to be the star. The more moments they have in front of their peers and others, the more capable they will become in commanding the leading role in their own lives.

Parents Add the Magical Ingredient

Applying the formula of success should not be a solo journey for youth. The magical ingredient that unlocks the radiance contained within every child is a meaningful bond with parents/guardians/protecting adults. Teenagers who are attempting to stretch their wings and explore new freedoms still cherish relationships with respected adults. The attention that caring adults shower on youth is the nutrition they need to flourish.